Welcome Speeches and Responses

Welcome Speeches and Responses

Herschel H. Hobbs
COMPILER

Baker Books
A Division of Baker Book House Co.
Grand Rapids, Michigan 49516

Contents

Welcome Speeches

Responses

Welcome Speeches

1

Welcome to Ministers
and Other Church Workers

New Pastor and Family

Today we welcome a new pastor and his family into our fellowship.

With God's guidance we have invited you, Reverend _____, to become the shepherd of this flock. We have asked you and your family to break ties with another church to come to us. It is our firm resolve to live and work with you so that soon the same intimate ties of Christian love will bind us together as pastor and people.

In asking you to become the shepherd of this church, we have given you a tremendous responsibility. We ask you to be our pastor, rejoicing with us when we rejoice and weeping with us when we weep. When we look at you from the pews, it will be with the unuttered cry, "Sir, we would see Jesus." We ask that you will make us "wise unto salvation," that you will teach us, reprove us, correct us, and instruct us in all things pertaining to righteousness. We pray that you will be God's overseer as you lead us in carrying out the work of the Lord. We know that you will be an example to us in both word and deed.

In turn, we are also assuming certain obligations. We shall take you and your family into our hearts. We shall respect your rights as a family. We shall keep you informed about our specific needs. Our hearts will be open to receive the messages which God gives through you. By our prayers, words and deeds we shall encourage you as your fellow workers.

In so doing, it is our prayer that before long we shall come to know that depth of love and fellowship between pastor and people expressed in the words of another pastor, John Fawcett:

> Blest be the tie that binds
> Our hearts in Christian love;
> The fellowship of kindred minds
> Is like to that above.
>
> Before our Father's throne
> We pour our ardent prayers;
> Our fears, our hopes, our aims are one,
> Our comforts and our cares.
>
> We share our mutual woes,
> Our mutual burdens bear;
> And often for each other flows
> The sympathizing tear.
>
> When we asunder part,
> It gives us inward pain;
> But we shall still be joined in heart,
> And hope to meet again.

Wife of a New Pastor

It is a great privilege to welcome the wife of our new pastor, _____.

The success of a pastorate depends on the pastor's wife. John Ruskin once wrote, "The buckling on of a knight's armor by his lady's hand was not a mere caprice of romantic fashion. It is the type of an eternal truth that the soul's armor is never set to the heart unless a woman's hand has braced it, and it is only when she braces it loosely that the honor of manhood fails."

Our pastor is one of God's knights; he wears spiritual armor. The success of his mission depends largely on his wife. With her love, counsel, prayers, and encouragement, she strengthens his armor.

Your love for your husband is tempered by your love for God. We trust that your love will be even richer and stronger because of our love for you.

We do not expect you to do the impossible. Your first duty, like ours, is to your family and your home. We shall not ask you to do more in the church than we are willing to do. But in the mutual love which we all share for our homes, our church, and our Lord, we shall join our hearts and our hands.

> Oh, how skilful grows the hand
> That obeyeth love's command;
> It is the heart and not the brain
> That to the highest doth attain,
> And he who follows love's behest
> Far exceedeth all the rest.

—*Henry Wadsworth Longfellow*

Former Pastor

(By Present Pastor)

It is my pleasure, on your behalf, to welcome to this pulpit a man who has served you faithfully and well. I do not need to tell you his name, for you know him and love him.

God has endowed you with a great capacity to love. I rejoice in the love which you have for Brother _____. If you did not love him, I would be afraid that you could not love me. The fact that he is so dear to your hearts confirms that you love me as well.

In a sense, when Paul spoke to the Ephesian elders, he was speaking as a former pastor (Acts 20:17ff.). I would like to direct these words to our guest for this hour. As we recall your labors as the pastor of this church, several things come to mind.

You have served the Lord in great humility. You have counseled with compassion, as in times of trial you have been called upon to declare the whole counsel of God. Without reservation, you have proclaimed the gospel of grace, calling for repentance and faith in our Lord Jesus Christ.

Knowing that Christ purchased your flock with his own blood, you have fed them as a shepherd. You have been God's overseer as you directed and led them in abundant labors for the Lord. Among this people your example has been a living parable of our Lord's words, "It is more blessed to give than to receive."

The fruits of your labor live on. We have endeavored to build on the foundation of your ministry. The blessings of God upon us today flow from your abiding labor of love. You planted, we have endeavored to water, and God gives the increase.

So with gratitude and pleasure too deep for words to express, I welcome you once again as we take you to our hearts. You are a beloved brother, a fellow laborer in the Lord, and a friend!

Former Pastor's Wife

Proverbs 18:22 acknowledges that "he who finds a wife finds what is good and receives favor from the LORD." It is my privilege to welcome someone who personifies this biblical truth.

You made the parsonage a refuge from the many trials and cares of a busy ministry. You shared your husband's dreams and his problems. Your wise counsel was reflected in the effectiveness of his pulpit ministry. You were a mother—and sometimes a father, too.

To paraphrase someone else's words: You were the pastor's silent partner. You were not "called," but you came, not "installed" yet you served. You were an "ambassador-without-portfolio." You were "104 sermons a year"—on the listening end. You were our pastor's "beloved critic, counselor, confronter." You had "all the problems a minister has—plus him!" You were "wife, mother, cook, laundress, seamstress, chauffeur—the Chancellor of the Exchequer—purchasing agent *par excellence.*" You were a woman with stars in your eyes and your hands in the dish pan.*

*See "What Is a Minister's Wife?" Mrs. H. D. Brown, copyright 1959 by Outlook Publishers.

You were always available without being pushy. You listened to our problems, yet kept our confidences inviolate. You lived quietly, yet you made an impact upon our lives.

So with joy we welcome you here once again. You may be our former pastor's wife, but you are our friend forever.

New Minister of Religious Education and Family

Teaching is fundamental to religion. In the Old Testament, God commands the children of Israel to teach: "Assemble the people—men, women and children, and the aliens living in your towns—so they can listen and learn to fear the LORD your God and follow carefully all the words of this law. Their children, who do not know this law, must hear it and learn to fear the LORD your God as long as you live in the land . . ." (Deut. 31:12–13).

Jesus was known as a teacher. He commissioned his disciples to teach all nations. Our church is also committed to a teaching ministry, using the Bible as our textbook.

In the providence of God we have invited _____ to direct our program of religious education. It is our privilege to welcome him and his family today.

We do not ask that you work *for* us but *with* us. Our task is your task. Your problems will be our concern. When we succeed, we shall rejoice with you; when we fail, we shall not ask that you bear all the blame.

We are willing people; we do not need to be driven

16

but led. Our hearts are large; we love our pastor, and we shall also love you. We shall not look upon you as a competitor but as a companion. As Aaron helped his brother, Moses, you will complement the ministry of your Christian brother, our pastor.

In receiving you as our co-laborer we promise you our prayers. We are ready to submit our time and talents as instruments of righteousness to be made more useful in your hands. We do not ask you to do our work, but to show us how we can do it better.

We know that the field is "white unto harvest," and we recognize that the "laborers are few." We join you in prayer that the Lord of the harvest will send forth laborers into his harvest. We trust that God will answer our prayers through you.

New Minister of Music and Family

Herbert Spencer once said that "music must rank as the highest of fine arts—as the one which, more than any other, ministers to human welfare." Music is the universal language of the soul. It expresses the deepest longings of the human heart. By it man's noblest aspirations find expression. It comforts in sorrow, it exhilarates in joy, it summons to duty.

The Christian religion is a singing religion. It was with joyful song that the angelic choir announced the birth of Christ. Jesus and his disciples sang a song before they went to the Mount of Olives. Paul admonishes us to ". . . be filled with the Spirit. Speak to one another with psalms, hymns and spiritual songs. Sing and make music in your heart to the Lord" (Eph. 5:19).

17

Our church has called _____ to serve as our minister of music. Today we open our hearts to welcome him and his family.

We are placing in your hands one of the most vital ministries of our church. We entrust our children to you, that under your guidance they may come to know the place of music in the worship service. We do not expect you to make us all sweet singers. We only ask that under your guidance we might gain a deeper appreciation for music. We pray that you will help us to become known as a singing church, where gospel music complements gospel teaching and preaching.

As we blend our voices, hearts, and hands, may they produce a symphony of praise to God.

Minister as Civic Club Speaker

Some years ago, an American railroad adopted the policy of issuing, upon request, an annual pass to any pastor whose church was located along the railroad's right-of-way. The railroad believed that its property was only as safe as the character of the people through whose communities it ran.

It is in this same spirit that we welcome Reverend _____ as the speaker for our club today.

Our club is dedicated to improving this city. This makes us co-laborers with our guest speaker. We remember the words of the Bible: man does not live on bread alone, but on every word that comes from the mouth of God. What is property if it becomes an end unto itself? What value is collateral without character? Indeed, what good will it be for a man if he gains the whole world, yet forfeits his soul in the process?

We are not here to be entertained. We did not invite you merely to speak to our minds, though you doubtless have some words of wisdom. It is our desire that you bring us a message from God. We want to hear words of eternal truth set in the context of our present needs. We want to realize the presence of God. "Where cross the crowded ways of life; where sound the cries of race and clan; above the noise of selfish strife"—through you—we want to hear the voice of Christ.

New Sunday School Superintendent

(Or Other Church Officer)

As we begin this new church year, we are happy to welcome as the new superintendent of our Sunday school, _____.

You have been chosen by our church for this work. Your fellow members have expressed their confidence in you. We realize, however, that you cannot do this work alone. We have given you leadership; we also pledge our "followship." In so doing, we would give you three admonitions.

First, *trust in yourself.* Shakespeare once wrote, "Our doubts are traitors and make us lose the good we oft might win by fearing to attempt." Ralph Waldo Emerson reminds us that "self-trust is the essence of heroism."

Second, *trust your fellow members.* Emerson said,

19

"Trust men and they will be true to you; treat them greatly and they will show themselves great."

Third, and most important of all, *trust in God*. "But be sure to fear the LORD and serve him faithfully with all your heart; consider what great things he has done for you" (1 Sam. 12:24).

> One there lives whose guardian eye
> Guides our earthly destiny;
> One there lives, who, Lord of all,
> Keeps His children lest they fall;
> Pass we, then, in love and praise,
> Trusting Him through all our days,
> Free from doubt and faithless sorrow,
> God provideth for the morrow.
>
> —*Reginald Heber*

New Associate Pastor and Family

It is a great privilege to welcome our new associate pastor, Reverend _____ and his family. The Lord has led us to invite you and your family to become fellow laborers in this church.

Your very title expresses the special relationship that you will share with our pastor. As an *associate* you will be especially associated with our pastor, working with him in every phase of this church's ministry. You will be his "second self" as you serve with and alongside him. As a *pastor* you will, under his direction, be an undershepherd of this flock.

As we love our pastor and his family, we shall also love you. In the Song of Solomon we read, "and his banner over me is love" (2:4). God's love in us, our love for him, and our love for one another will be the banner under which we shall do our work.

> Love is the filling from one's own
>   Another's cup;
> Love is the daily lying down
>   And taking up;
> A choosing of the stony path
>   Through each new day
> That other feet may tread with ease
>   A smoother way.
> Love is not blind, but looks abroad
>   Through other eyes;
> And asks not, "Must I give?" but
>   "May I sacrifice?"
> Love hides its grief, that other hearts
>   And lips may sing;
> And burdened walks, that other lives
>   May buoyant wing.
> Hast thou a love like this
>   Within thy soul?
> 'Twill crown thy life with bliss
>   When thou dost reach the goal.

—*Anonymous*

Newly-ordained Minister

I am happy to welcome our newly-ordained Brother _____ into the fellowship of the gospel ministry.

God never honors a church more than when he reaches down and places his hand on one of its young members. Through the years it has been our privilege not only to lead you to the Lord but to guide you as you have grown in his grace. Your call to the ministry is one of God's seals of approval upon our church.

Believing that you have been called by God to the ministry, our church has set you apart through ordination for this work. In so doing, we have assumed a great obligation. We are obliged to pray for you and to stand by you as you continue to grow in Christ.

On behalf of our church, I would exhort you to: "preach the word" (2 Tim. 4:2); "endure hardship . . . like a good soldier of Christ Jesus" (2 Tim. 2:3); "do the work of an evangelist, discharge all the duties of your ministry" (2 Tim. 4:5); "see to it that you complete the work you have received in the Lord" (Col. 4:17).

I welcome you as my fellow soldier to this calling of God in Christ Jesus. It is not an easy life. Paul reminds us: "But we have this treasure in jars of clay to show that this all-surpassing power is from God and not from us. We are hard pressed on every side, but not crushed; perplexed, but not in despair; persecuted, but not abandoned; struck down, but not destroyed. We always carry around in our body the death of Jesus, so that the life of Jesus may also be revealed in our body" (2 Cor. 4:7–10). But God says, " 'My grace is sufficient for you, for my power is made perfect in weakness.' Therefore I will boast all the more gladly about my weaknesses, so that Christ's power may rest on me" (2 Cor. 12:9).

It is not the easiest of callings. But it *is* the greatest. I welcome you, therefore, in the name of him who called us to the ministry.

2

Welcome to Visitors

Visitors in a Worship Service

—1—

One of the most blessed moments in any hour of worship is when we pause to welcome those who are visiting with us. Our prayer is that the Holy Spirit will unite our hearts so that we become one worshiping body bowed before God's throne of grace.

If you are a visitor, please raise your hand. One of our ushers will give you a packet of information to help you become familiar with our church. Included is a card which we would like you to fill out so that we can become better acquainted with you. You will also find a red ribbon to wear which will identify you as a visitor after the service. We want to make this general welcome a personal one.

Moses once said to Hobab, "We are setting out for the place about which the LORD said, 'I will give it to you.' Come with us and we will treat you well . . ."

(Num. 10:29). We will do you good, and you will do us good.

We want you to be more than visitors to our church. We invite you to become members of our family of faith. Our prayer for you is that today you will make our church your church, and our Savior your Savior!

—2—

The Bible says a lot about the fellowship of worship. We are warned not to give up meeting together (Heb. 10:25). In 1 Chronicles 16:29 we read, "Ascribe to the LORD the glory due his name. Bring an offering and come before him; worship the LORD in the splendor of his holiness."

Thomas Carlyle once asked, "What greater calamity can fall upon a nation than the loss of worship?" But the need for divine worship is not just national; it is also personal. The psalmist cries, "As the deer pants for streams of water, so my soul pants for you, O God" (Ps. 42:1).

You have come here with your hopes and dreams, your cares and tears, your guilt, and your prayers. As you worship with us, may you realize your fondest hopes and dreams. May your cares be removed, and your tears dried. May your guilt be cleansed. May your prayers be answered.

> May the grace of Christ our Saviour
> And the Father's boundless love,
> With the Holy Spirit's favor,
> Rest upon us from above.
>
> Thus may we abide in union
> With each other and the Lord,
> And possess in sweet communion,
> Joys which earth cannot afford.
>
> —John Newton

Visitors in Sunday School

A wise man once wrote, "A man of many companions may come to ruin, but there is a friend who sticks closer than a brother" (Prov. 18:24). It is in this spirit that we welcome our visitors.

Our deepest desire is to be a friendly Sunday school. We want you to be more than visitors; we want you to be our friends.

This church is a spiritual home. The welcome mat is out. Even before people knock we want to open the door to our hearts, to receive them into the warmth of our love. We greet you not as a mere formality, but in the confidence that our words express what we feel in our hearts.

The primary purpose of our Sunday school is not a social one, yet we enjoy Christian fellowship together. It is not merely to impart knowledge, though we do seek to unveil the truth using the Bible as our textbook. Our primary purpose is to introduce you to our divine friend, Jesus Christ.

Some of you already have him as your friend. It is our desire to help you become a closer friend as you learn and practice the things which he has taught us. For those who do not know this friend who is closer than a brother, we pray that through our friendship you *will* come to know him.

Soon we shall go to our respective classes. If you have not found yours, we shall be happy to help you. The words of welcome which I speak for us collectively will soon be spoken to you personally. Our prayer is that you will "go home to your family and tell them how much the Lord has done for you . . ." (Mark 5:19).

Visitors in the Baptist Training Union

(Christian Endeavor, etc.)

An important part of this meeting is welcoming our visitors.

The purpose of this Sunday evening gathering is to make ourselves better Christians and church members. Meeting in small groups, we can get to know one another more intimately and can also learn by doing. Paul writes, "Do your best to present yourself to God as one approved, a workman who does not need to be ashamed and who correctly handles the word of truth" (2 Tim. 2:15).

We are saved to serve. A man can cut down a tree with a dull axe, but the task is much easier with a sharp one. We can be more effective in our service for Christ if our minds are sharp, our hands are skillful, and our hearts are concerned.

As we study our missionary program, we learn about doctrinal beliefs, worship together, improve our skills in spiritual service, and enlarge our vision. Most of all, we endeavor to actively serve Christ.

Following this meeting, we shall attend the evening worship service. There, in a larger fellowship and under the leadership of our pastor, we shall worship, pray, and help sinners come to know our Savior.

Therefore, we welcome you as visitors, hoping that you will join us so we all might be enriched and encouraged in the Lord.

Visitors in Women's Missionary Society

We are delighted to have visitors with us today.

Donald Grant Mitchell says that a woman without

religion is "a flame without heat, a rainbow without color, a flower without perfume." A woman *with* religion is a flame casting the light of God's love into dark places, a colorful rainbow shining with promise through the storms of life, a flower whose sweet perfume of love and devotion delights our heavenly Father.

God worked through Deborah when his people were oppressed and cried out for deliverance. God used Esther to save his people from destruction. God chose Mary to give birth to Jesus when he became flesh and dwelt among us. Women were the last to see Jesus on the cross and the first to proclaim his resurrection.

The Book of Luke recognizes the place of women in Jesus' earthly ministry. As Jesus went about preaching the gospel, "the Twelve were with him, and also some women . . . helping to support them out of their own means" (Luke 8:1–3). Each of these women had been specially blessed by Jesus. In turn, they sought to share him with others.

Through our Women's Missionary Society we endeavor to teach, promote, and support missionary work around the world. We welcome you to our fellowship. We invite you to join with us as we help you and you help us in the cause of the gospel.

Visitors in Men's Brotherhood

Someone has said that the ancient Greeks "stole" all of our original thoughts. In that sense, about 500 B.C. Aeschylus stole my original thought for tonight. He said, "Pleasantest of all ties is the tie of host and guest." Speaking for our Men's Brotherhood to our guests, let me say that ours is a pleasant tie indeed.

It is the tie of fellowship, faith, and spiritual unity. It is the tie of service forged by self-denial for the common good.

The true goal of manhood is to be a follower of Christ. To walk in his footsteps demands commitment, courage, conquest, and sacrifice. To be healthy and vigorous, God's work must have such faithful men at its center.

Our group is built on the belief that faith is a manly virtue. However, it does not exist only for men. Instead, it endeavors to get every man to support every phase of our church's work.

To that end we welcome you. To that task we challenge you. Let us be united in that indissoluble bond of Christian service as we work together for the Lord.

Visitors in Midweek Prayer Service

—1—

In Christian love we welcome our visitors to this hour of prayer. Someone has said that the midweek prayer service is an island of refuge in the midst of the stormy sea separating our Sundays. We welcome you to this refuge, remembering that we ". . . should always pray and not give up" (Luke 18:1).

—2—

You can judge the popularity of a church by the Sunday morning congregation, the popularity of its pastor by the Sunday evening congregation, and the popularity of the Lord by the Wednesday evening congregation. Although our visitors claim neither our church nor our pastor as theirs, they *do* claim our Lord as their Lord. We welcome you in his name!

—3—

We welcome our visitors to our midweek prayer service.

Victor Hugo once wrote, "There are moments when whatever be the attitude of the body, the soul is on its knees." Let us come, both body and soul, before our heavenly Father.

—4—

During the darkest hours of the Civil War, Abraham Lincoln said, "I have been driven many times to my knees by the overwhelming conviction that I had nowhere else to go. My own wisdom, and that of all about me, seemed insufficient for the day."

We, too, live in troubled times when only prayer can help. To this service, therefore, we welcome not only our members but especially our visitors. Let us pray as we live, and live as we pray.

Visitors in Midweek Church Dinner

It is with delight that we welcome our guests to our midweek dinner.

If you would really know a family, you must see it not only when it is dressed to receive guests. You must observe it as it goes about its daily routine.

A cynic once criticized the church for investing so heavily in property used only once a week. Such criticism cannot be leveled against our church. To borrow a thought from Shakespeare, our "task does not divide the Sunday from the week."

Tonight you see us as a family gathered around a table. Soon you will join with us in prayer, humbly baring our souls before God.

Wednesday night is the halfway point between Sundays. It is a time when we replenish our failing strength. It is a moment when we lift our eyes from the rugged path of daily living to God.

We welcome you here. We want to know you and to be known by you. We trust that our welcome will warm your hearts. It is our hope that you will come again—and often. We pray that you will be with us on the Lord's day, that you will become more than guests, that you will join our family of faith.

We have been made richer by your presence tonight. We shall be enriched indeed if you join us in knowing and doing the will of Christ.

Visitors in General Church Dinner

Many of you have brought guests to our church dinner this evening. We extend to each a hearty welcome.

Jesus attended banquets so frequently that his enemies accused him of being a drunkard and a glutton. Jesus knew the wholesome fellowship of men, women, and children gathered around a table. But for him such gatherings were not an end unto themselves; they were means to an end, occasions for teaching.

We, too, see this dinner hour as a means to an end. It is a time of worship and fellowship. It is a time of information and inspiration. It is a time for renewing old friendships and forging new ones.

We hope that being with us is such a delightful experience that you will join us in the full life of our church. So in the name of him who often sat at the banquet table, and who sits with us even now, we welcome you.

Military Personnel

We are honored to have in our service today members of our armed forces.

There is no conflict between being soldiers of our nation and soldiers of the cross. The New Testament often expresses spiritual truth using military metaphors.

Some great military figures have been faithful followers of Christ. The Duke of Wellington said, "The Lord's prayer contains the sum total of religion and morals." George Washington said, "Providence has at all times been my only dependence, for all other resources seem to have failed us." Robert E. Lee was a man of deep, abiding faith. On the eve of one of his greatest battles, Stonewall Jackson, a Presbyterian elder, wrote a letter to his pastor, enclosing his church contribution.

As military personnel, you are the watchmen on the walls of our nation. However, you recognize the truth spoken by the psalmist: ". . . Unless the LORD watches over the city, the watchmen stand guard in vain" (Ps. 127:1b).

So we welcome you to our service today. We shall keep you in our prayers. We shall remember your

31

loved ones at home. And we shall fight by your side as soldiers of the Lord so that the Prince of Peace may reign in all nations and over all men.

Visitors in Revival Service

A revival service without visitors is like a three-piece treasure map with two pieces missing. Therefore, we are especially pleased to welcome our visitors to this service.

Generally speaking, a revival meeting has a threefold purpose. It is a time of renewal for our own members. It is a time for a special effort to involve other Christians in the full life of our church. It is a period of serious endeavor to reach the unsaved for Christ.

To our visitors who are followers of Christ, but who have no church home in our city, we extend a cordial invitation to join us, blessing your lives as you strengthen ours. For other visitors who have never professed faith in Jesus as Savior, we pray that tonight you will yield to the Holy Spirit.

Someone has suggested that to achieve true success in life, we must discover what God is doing in a given time and dedicate ourselves to his purpose and will.

History shows that God moves mysteriously in revival movements. The English revival led by John Wesley is credited with saving England from the horrors of the French Revolution. In America the Great Awakening challenged deism and infidelity. We believe that God is moving today to lead us through a time when the fate of civilization seems to depend on man's judgment and will.

Therefore, we welcome you in the hope that you will join with us in an old revival song:

Revive us again; fill each heart with thy love;
May each soul be rekindled with fire from above.

—William P. Mackay

3

Welcome to New Church Members

Transfers from Another Church

—1—

We are happy to welcome you as new members of our church. You have come *from* a great church *to* a great church.

A church is not judged by its size but by its spirit. It is not measured by its wealth but by its willingness to fulfill God's will. In that sense we can claim to be a great church.

Hebrews 11 is one of the most inspiring chapters in the New Testament. It talks about God's heroes of faith, closing with these words: "These were all commended for their faith, yet none of them received what had been promised. God had planned something better for us so that only together with us would they be made perfect."

Essentially, the writer of Hebrews is saying that the *degree of our faithfulness* is a demonstration of the *fruit of our forefathers' faith.* Our church is what it is today because of those who went before us.

As new members of our church, then, we would remind you of

> A noble army, men and boys,
>   The matron and the maid,
> Around the Saviour's throne rejoice,
>   In robes of light arrayed.
>
> They climbed the steep ascent of heaven
>   Through peril, toil, and pain;
> O God, to us may grace be given
>   To follow in their train!

> —*Reginald Heber*

—2—

The best part of our worship service is welcoming new members into our fellowship. By the grace of God in Christ Jesus, and under the guidance of the Holy Spirit, you have decided to join this church.

In receiving you we assume certain responsibilities. We shall minister to your spiritual needs. We shall endeavor to strengthen you as we keep you in our prayers. We shall seek to comfort you in difficult times, and to rejoice with you in good times. We shall guide you as you continue to grow in the grace and knowledge of Christ.

But in receiving you we also place great responsibilities on you. Our church will be no better than you are. Its witness depends on your witness. Its stewardship will be limited or enhanced by the measure of your stewardship.

You will carry with you this church's good name. Wherever you go it will go. Whatever you do it will do. Men will judge this church by your consecration or lack of it.

On behalf of our church I extend my hand to you as a token of our fellowship and love, of our pledge to assume the responsibilities which are placed on us. If you, in turn, offer your fellowship and love, and accept the obligations which your coming places on you, will you place your hand in mine?

May Christ, the Head of the church, and the Holy Spirit who indwells every believer, witness our pledges, and empower us to fulfill them.

New Christians

—1—

This is an awesome moment. Once again the Holy Spirit has done a wondrous work, and we are privileged to welcome a new Christian into our fellowship.

You have repented of your sins and in faith have confessed Christ as your Savior. From being dead in trespasses and sin you have come to know new life in Christ Jesus.

Among the ancient Greeks and Romans unwanted babies were abandoned to die either from exposure or as the prey of wild animals. Such a practice was called *infanticide.* Even worse is the modern practice of *spiritual infanticide,* whereby we neglect those who are babes in Christ.

Our responsibility for you has just begun. We welcome you to our hearts. We want to give you every opportunity to develop into the kind of Christian God would have you to be.

In that spirit we receive you today. Our prayer for each is found in 3 John 2: "Dear Friend, I pray that you may enjoy good health and that all may go well with you, even as your soul is getting along well."

—2—

It is a joyful occasion when a baby is born. But the joy is tempered by the tremendous responsibility which God places on the baby's family. A baby must be fed, clothed, loved, and guided.

Our joy here is also tempered joy. Here is a babe who must be fed, first on the sincere milk of the Word, and then on the strong meat of the Bible's teachings. The baby must be clothed with Christian character and trained in righteousness. The baby must be loved with the love of Christ and nurtured as he or she grows in Christ.

So, welcome into the household of faith! You have been born again into God's kingdom. You will be baptized into the fellowship of his church. You have not ended your spiritual pilgrimage, you have only begun it. In the words of Sir Walter Raleigh may you say,

> Give me my scallop-shell of quiet,
> My staff of faith to walk upon,
> My scrip of joy, immortal diet,
> My bottle of salvation,
> My gown of glory, hope's true gage,
> And thus I'll take my pilgrimage.

4

Welcome to Guest Speakers

Guest Minister

Today we are fortunate to welcome Reverend
_____ as our guest minister.

John Greenleaf Whittier, in "Sunset on the Bear-
camp," wrote,

> Touched by a light that hath no name,
> A glory never sung,
> Aloft on sky and mountain wall
> Are God's great pictures hung.

The gospel is God's greatest picture. It portrays his
love and grace given to a lost world. Like all great
pictures, it has many facets; each perspective presents
a message from God to the hearts of men.

Our guest minister today will help us see this picture in a new light—hues and textures we never saw
before. As Paul says, "And we, who with unveiled
faces all reflect the Lord's glory, are being transformed

into his likeness with ever-increasing glory, which comes from the Lord, who is the Spirit" (2 Cor. 3:18).

To that end we welcome you as our guest minister.

Guest Evangelist

We are happy to welcome to our church Reverend _____, our guest evangelist during these days of evangelistic outreach.

We have organized, publicized, and prayed, in the confidence that this might be a time of self-renewal as well as a time to proclaim the saving grace of God in Christ.

We do not expect you to bring a revival to us. We only ask that you lead us in humbling ourselves before God that *he* might revive us. We shall pray for you as you preach to us. We shall seek to bring before you those who need to hear the gospel, to be redeemed from sin and guided into new life in Christ Jesus.

This is not *your* revival, but *ours.* Since we have asked you to leave your work in order to help us do ours, we shall take time from our daily responsibilities to be present at the services, and shall make an effort to bring those who need to come with us.

So, welcome, beloved comrade. And people of God, as

Soldiers of Christ, arise, and put your armor on,
Strong in the strength which God supplies through
   His eternal Son;
Strong in the Lord of hosts, and in His mighty power,
Who in the strength of Jesus trusts is
   more than conqueror.

—Charles Wesley

39

Guest Soloist

—1—

We welcome _____ as our guest soloist today.

Henry Wadsworth Longfellow once wrote,

> God sent his singers on earth
> With songs of gladness and mirth
> That they might touch the hearts of men
> And bring them back to Heaven again.

God has sent you to us. He has given you the ability to sing, and has placed a song in your heart. Through music, the universal language of the soul, God will speak to us through you.

—2—

On your behalf I am privileged to welcome _____, our guest soloist today.

Thomas Carlyle once wrote, "Music is well said to be the speech of angels." An angel is a messenger from God. So you are God's messenger to us. Through your ministry God will speak to our hearts. We shall tune not only our ears but our hearts to your song.

Guest Evangelistic Soloist

We are happy to welcome _____ to our revival.

Music has always played a vital role in great revival movements. The Wesleyan revivals needed John Wesley, but they also needed his brother, Charles. Dwight L. Moody was a great preacher, but Ira D. Sankey was also essential to the success of those revival campaigns. One can hardly imagine Billy Sunday without Homer Rodeheaver.

In our revival, we have emphasized singing as well as preaching. Indeed, both are essential in the proclamation of the gospel. Great singing inspires great preaching, and preaching gives added meaning to the gospel set to music.

As fire softens metal for the stroke of the hammer, so the warmth of music prepares hearts for the preaching of the gospel.

May your music soften our hearts to the impact of the gospel, and bend them to the will of God. Paul writes, "I will sing with my spirit, but I will also sing with my mind" (1 Cor. 14:15b).

How many of us ever stop to think
Of music as a wondrous magic link
With God; taking sometimes the place of prayer
When words have failed us 'neath the weight of care.
Music, that knows no country, race or creed,
But gives to each according to his need.

—*Anonymous*

Guest Missionary

We are delighted to welcome Reverend _____, one of our faithful missionaries, to our service today.

When Paul and Barnabas returned from their first missionary journey, they "gathered the church together and reported all that God had done through them and how he had opened the door of faith to the Gentiles" (Acts 14:27). In a sense we are doing the same thing today.

Edward Everett Hale would call our guest one of the "nameless saints." Most people do not recognize his worth. But he is known to us, and, most of all, to God.

You are not alone in your work. Your work is our work. You are an extension of ourselves in the service of our Lord. Your commitment must be equaled by our dedication to prayer and giving.

We welcome you to our hearts. We look forward to your message of encouragement.

Guest Speaker at a Father – Son Banquet

We are happy to have _____ as our speaker. His greatest qualification is that he is both a son and a father.

The father–son relationship is a special one. God the Father sent his Son to die for our sins. The relationship between a father and a son, then, takes on the aura of heaven.

In such a relationship there is a great need for understanding. A man once sought to discredit a doctor in the eyes of his son. He said, "Did you know that your father takes sick people, straps them to a table, knocks them out, and then cuts them up?" The son said, "Mister, I don't know what *you* are talking about, but I *do* know my dad!"

We hope that your message will help us to understand each other.

Guest Speaker at a Mother – Daughter Banquet

We are honored to have _____ as our speaker tonight. She will not be lecturing to us out of books, but will be speaking from her heart. Her message is not theory but fact. She does not merely *listen* to the Word—she *does what it says.*

A message may be excellent. However, it is effective only if it is heard. Let us listen carefully, and take _____'s words into our hearts. What we hear is not only going to affect us as mothers and daughters; it will influence the whole of our lives.

We are honored by your presence; we shall be blessed by your words.

Guest Speaker at a Stewardship Banquet

—1—

We are fortunate to have _____ as the speaker for our annual stewardship banquet. He is a man who understands stewardship, practices it in his own life, and is capable of challenging us to do the same.

The Bible says, "Now it is required that those who have been given a trust must prove faithful" (1 Cor. 4:2). Stewardship involves the whole of life. It recognizes God as the giver of life, and challenges us to use it for his glory. In this sense stewardship is the most widely taught concept in God's Word.

Henry Ward Beecher once said, "Men are often like knives with many blades; they know how to open one and only one; all the rest are buried in the handle, and they are no better than they would have been if they had been made with but one blade. Many men use but one or two faculties out of the score with which they are endowed."

We must think about stewardship. We do not fully belong to God until he controls all that we are and have. To that end we welcome our guest speaker, that he might challenge us to love God and to obey his will. Through his presence tonight may we all be led to say,

> We give Thee but thine own, whate'er
>   the gift may be;
> All that we have is thine alone, a
>   trust, O Lord, from Thee.
>
> May we Thy bounties thus as
>   stewards true receive,
> And gladly as Thou blessest us,
>   to Thee our first fruits give.
>
> The captive to release, to God
>   the lost to bring,
> To teach the way of life and peace,
>   it is a Christ-like thing.
>
> And we believe Thy Word, though
>   dim our faith may be;
> Whate'er for Thee we do, O Lord,
>   we do it unto Thee.
>
> —*William W. How*

—2—

We are happy to welcome _____ as the speaker for our annual stewardship dinner.

Some of the greatest teachings of the Bible concern

stewardship. Covetousness is a common sin, so God has repeatedly warned us about it. On the other hand, because wise stewardship is the key to an abundant life, God has fully taught us about it.

We need to be reminded of the broad nature of stewardship, and must learn to use our material possessions responsibly. Soon we shall be making our annual pledges to the church. Everything that we do, both here and around the world, depends on the responses that we make.

_____ knows about stewardship, both from the teachings of the Bible and from personal experience. May his coming lead us all to sing

> All things are Thine; no gift have we,
> Lord of all gifts, to offer Thee,
> And hence, with grateful hearts today,
> Thine own before Thy feet we lay.
>
> *—John G. Whittier*

Guest Speaker in Sunday School

We are pleased to present Brother _____ as our guest speaker. Before going to our classes, we need to spend a few moments in worship.

Henry Wadsworth Longfellow once wrote

> Where'er a noble deed is wrought,
> Where'er is spoken a noble thought,
>   Our hearts in glad surprise
>   To higher levels rise.

A part of worship is meditation. Brother _____ is well qualified to lead us in it. He

45

knows us, he knows our church, but most of all he knows the Lord.

Guest Speaker in Women's Missionary Society

We are happy to have _____ with us as our guest speaker.

Many years ago Emily Dickinson wrote,

> To see her is a picture,
> To hear her is a tune. . . .

We may well apply these words to our guest today.

However, the picture which we see is not because _____ is beautiful only on the outside; she also has depth and beauty of soul. The tune which we hear is a symphony of her attributes and attitudes, dedicated to God.

You bring something which the Lord has placed on your heart. We look forward to hearing from you.

Guest Speaker at Men's Fellowship Dinner

It is my unique privilege at this time to present as our guest speaker, _____.

The purpose of this dinner is for men to have fellowship with men. Borrowing a thought from Arthur Davison Ficke, it is an hour when from our faces "veils pass, and laughing fellowship glows warm."

But this is more than a time for food and fellowship. It is a time for information and inspiration—for the fellowship of ideas.

To that end we have invited as our speaker some-

46

one who can not only entertain but also inform. We did not invite him because he is famous. We invited him because of his friendship. Oliver Wendell Holmes once wrote

> Fame is the scentless sunflower,
>   with gaudy crown of gold;
> But friendship is the breathing rose,
>   with sweets in every fold.

So, our friend, we extend a hearty welcome to you. You will do us good.

Guest Government Official

—1—

The greater and more prominent the speaker, the less one needs to say about him. Therefore, it is my pleasure to present to you the Honorable Mr. _____, (mayor of our city, governor of our state, senior United States senator from our state, judge of our district court, etc.).

—2—

It is my great pleasure to present our speaker for the evening, the Honorable Mr. _____.

Paul tells us that government has been established by God (Rom. 13). Public officials are God's servants to do us good.

In accepting the nomination for governor of New York, Grover Cleveland wrote, "Public officers are the servants and agents of the people, to execute the laws which the people have made." In his presidential inaugural address he added, "Your every voter, as surely as your chief magistrate, exercises a public trust." So all of us recognize a common heritage and obligation. We are free men in whose hands have been placed the dignities and responsibilities of liberty.

In recognition of our trust, we welcome you.

Minister of Another Denomination

This is a significant service for all of us. It is our privilege to welcome as our guest Reverend _____, pastor of the _____ Church of our city.

God has made us all individuals. As such we do not view life through the same eyes. Nonetheless, our hearts beat as one. In the words of John Wesley: "If thy heart is as my heart, give me thy hand."

No one was more sure about what he believed than Paul. Yet he also knew the broader fellowship of the gospel. From a prison in Rome he wrote to the church in Philippi, noting that Christ is preached in many ways (Phil. 1:18).

We are children of God, brethren in Christ. As a family is made up of different people yet is one in spirit, so we as children of God find unity in diversity.

We trust that in our fellowship in Christ today, and always, you may be blessed by us while we are fed by your words.

Minister of Another Nationality

We are happy to greet the Reverend _____ as our guest minister today.

One of the unique features of the Christian gospel is that God is not a tribal or national god. He is the God of all nations and of all men: "God so loved the world that he gave his one and only Son, that whoever believes in him shall not perish, but have eternal life" (John 3:16).

Standing on Mars Hill in Athens, Paul declared that "from one man he [God] made every nation of men, that they should inhabit the whole earth; and he determined the times set for them and the exact places where they should live. God did this so that men would seek him . . ." (Acts 17:26–27a).

The gospel of Christ knows no national boundaries. Its purpose is not to be conformed to any given age, but to transform men of every age. It has challenged every cultural and political philosophy. It has spoken to princes and peasants, servants and masters, scholars and simpletons. Its one message: "Believe in the Lord Jesus, and you will be saved . . ." (Acts 16:31). Its one goal: "The kingdom of the world has become the kingdom of our Lord and of his Christ; and he will reign for ever and ever" (Rev. 11:15).

Our guest today is a fellow patriot in the kingdom of God. He is a fellow soldier in the army of the Lord. Our mutual citizenship is in heaven.

We welcome you today both as a friend and a brother.

Minister of Another Race

It is our privilege to welcome as our guest today the Reverend _____.

Speaking to Cornelius, a Gentile, Peter, a Jew, declared, "I now realize how true it is that God does

49

not show favoritism but accepts men from every nation who fear him and do what is right" (Acts 10:34–35). In fact, Peter is saying that God does not judge a person by his race; "man looks at the outward appearance, but the LORD looks at the heart" (1 Sam. 16:7).

When God said, "This is my Son, whom I love; with him I am well pleased" (Matt. 3:17), he was not looking at the hue of his skin, the height of his cheekbones, the slant of his eyes, or the contour of his face. God was looking into Jesus' heart.

It is in this spirit that we welcome our Christian brother. Paul summarizes the matter for us: "You are all sons of God through faith in Christ Jesus. . . . There is neither Jew nor Greek, slave nor free, male nor female, for you are all one in Christ Jesus" (Gal. 3:26, 28).

Our prayer today is that God will speak through you.

Guest Denominational Leader

It is an honor to welcome to our church today the Reverend _____, executive secretary (bishop) of the Convention (Conference, Synod).

The work of our denomination is varied and widespread. Each church has its particular programs and interests. But beyond the local church's work is a larger, cooperative task. Our guest personifies that endeavor.

Such a person must have many abilities. He must be able to serve both the largest and the smallest churches. He must think in terms of both local congregations and the world. He must be both diplomat and administrator. He must deal in organizations without becoming an organizer. He must be a man of vision as well as of practical pursuits. He must keep his head in the clouds but his feet on the ground.

Our guest today is such a man. We look to him for a vision, a task, and a message from God.

5

Welcome to Church Conventions

District or State Convention

It is a privilege for our church to host the annual meeting of our district (state) convention. On behalf of our church, we welcome you. We place ourselves and our facilities at your disposal.

Soon we are going to receive reports about what God has done through us this past year. We trust that we shall truly " to God give the glory for great things he has done." While we rejoice in his goodness to us, we must be mindful of the responsibility which he places on us. Alexander MacLaren said, "Ability involves responsibility."

You have come with a serious purpose. Decisions will be made and plans initiated which will determine our witness here and throughout the world. Thomas Carlyle once said, "The man without a purpose is like a ship without a rudder—a waif, a nothing, a no man. Have a purpose in life, and, having it, throw such strength of mind and muscle into your works as God has given you."

Isaiah delivered this challenge to God's people: "Whether you turn to the right or to the left, your ears will hear a voice behind you, saying, 'This is the way; walk in it' " (Isa. 30:21). Our prayer for this gathering is that we shall hear God's voice and know his will and way.

National Convention

I am privileged to welcome the _____ Convention. We have done all that we can to make your stay here both pleasurable and memorable.

The work of this convention involves more than our nation. We need to remember places where the gospel is scarcely known. We need to hear the Macedonian cry, "Come over and help us!"

The media brings the world into our homes. Rapid travel makes distant people our neighbors. The advances of material science have exceeded our fondest—and, perhaps, worst—dreams. The destructive potential of modern nations is too terrible to imagine. But when the world is at its worst, the Christian must be at his best.

With Paul we acknowledge, "who is equal to such a task?" (2 Cor. 2:16) However, with him we can also say, ". . . my God will meet all your needs according to his glorious riches in Christ Jesus" (Phil. 4:19).

> We are living, we are dwelling in a
> grand and awful time,

In an age on ages telling; to be
  living is sublime.
Hark! the waking up of nations,
  hosts advancing to the fray;
Hark! what soundeth is creation's
  groaning for the latter day.

Will ye play, then? will ye dally
  far behind the battle line?
Up! it is Jehovah's rally; God's
  own arm hath need of thine.

Worlds are charging, heaven beholding;
  thou hast but an hour to fight;
Now, the blazoned cross unfolding, on,
  right onward for the right!

Sworn to yield, to waver, never; consecrated,
  born again;
Sworn to be Christ's soldiers ever, on!
  for Christ at least be men!
On! let all the soul within you for
  the truth's sake go abroad!
Strike! let every nerve and sinew tell
  on ages, tell for God.

—*A. Cleveland Coxe*

6

Welcome to Various Delegations

Delegation of Boy or Girl Scouts

(Or Other Youth Groups)

We welcome to our service a group of Boy Scouts (Girl Scouts, etc.) and their leaders.

For more than a half century, the object of the scouting movement has been to develop in boys and girls characters which are well pleasing to God.

Jesus would have been a Boy Scout had such a troop existed in Nazareth. He was familiar with nature and the messages it has to teach about God. He kept his body strong, his mind alert, and his character pure. He went about doing good. He developed woodworking skills. He had indomitable courage. He was kind to the weak, and sought to lend a helping hand with no thought of personal reward. "And Jesus grew in wisdom and stature, and in favor with God and men" (Luke 2:52).

Our church supports the scouting movement. It sponsors its work. Many of our members are involved in its program.

A scout is taught to worship. So you are at home in a service such as this. We welcome you in the name of him who said, "Let the little children come to me, and do not hinder them, for the kingdom of God belongs to such as these" (Mark 10:14).

An anonymous poet writes,

> God wants the boys, the merry, merry boys,
> The noisy boys, the funny boys,
>   The thoughtless boys;
> God wants the boys with all their joys
> That He as gold may make them pure,
> And teach them trials to endure,
>   His heroes brave
>   He'd have them be.
>   Fighting for truth
>   And purity,
>   God wants the boys!
>
> God wants the happy-hearted girls,
> The loving girls, the best of girls,
>   The worst of girls;
> God wants to make the girls His pearls,
> And so reflect His holy face,
> And bring to mind His wondrous grace,
>   That beautiful
>   The world may be,
>   And filled with love
>   And purity.
>   God wants the girls!

Delegation of Pastors

We are happy to have with us a group of pastors who are meeting in our city.

The Bible makes no distinction between pastors and laymen when it comes to their relationship with God. We are all sinners saved by grace. However, God has made the pastor a shepherd of souls, and his responsibility makes it all the more necessary that he should bow in worship before the One who gave him his ministry.

We welcome you as those who hunger for a new experience with the living God. As we pray we shall lift your congregations before the throne of grace. We shall remember your families. We send you from us strengthened for your present mission. We are blessed by your presence.

Delegation of Laymen

We are delighted to have with us a group of dedicated laymen from a sister church.

For several days they have been in our city to study our church program, hoping to get ideas which may be helpful to them in their own church. They have met with the pastor and the church staff. They have conferred with our deacons and with various church groups.

We have received more than we have given. Your presence with us dignifies the work of the Lord. That you would leave your own businesses and homes for this purpose testifies to your consecration and recognition of the importance of spiritual things.

And now we end your visit in worship. May we forget the *mechanics* and remember the *dynamics* of our service. May we be reminded that "unless the LORD builds the house, its builders labor in vain" (Ps. 127:1). It is "not by might nor by power, but by my Spirit, says the LORD almighty" (Zech. 4:6).

General Delegation

(4H, Future Homemakers, etc.)

We are honored by the presence of the _____ in our service.

From time to time it is our privilege to have various groups worship with us. We are happy that you have chosen to worship in our church.

Many organizations help our people live richer, fuller lives. With all of them we share a common cause. But *we* have a unique responsibility. The church of the Lord Jesus is given the responsibility of teaching men, women, and children how to worship.

True worship is more than just one hour each week spent in a church building. It is an attitude, a way of life. It recognizes that our souls need salvation, found in Christ alone. It recognizes that the body is the temple of the Holy Spirit. It realizes that though we may be out of God's house, we are never out of his presence.

So we welcome you in the name of him who died, rose again, and ever lives to make intercession for us before the throne of grace. May all of us enter God's house to worship, and depart to serve!

7

Dedications

New Church or Addition

—1—

One of the most solemn moments in Old Testament history is Solomon's prayer of dedication for the temple in Jerusalem (1 Kings 8:22–61). Let us use Solomon's words to dedicate this building to God:

> But will God really dwell on earth? The heavens, even the highest heaven, cannot contain you. How much less this temple I have built! Yet give attention to your servant's prayer and his plea for mercy, O LORD my God. Hear the cry and the prayer that your servant is praying in your presence this day. May your eyes be open toward this temple night and day, this place of which you said, 'My Name shall be there,' so that you will hear the prayer your servant prays toward this place. . . . Hear from heaven, your dwelling place, and when you hear, forgive (1 Kings 8:27–30). Amen.

We dedicate this building to *Christian fellowship.* The writer to the Hebrews admonishes us not to give up meeting together, "but let us encourage one another—and all the more as you see the Day approaching" (Heb. 10:25).

We dedicate it to *worship.* David says, "ascribe to the Lord the glory due his name. Bring an offering and come before him; worship the Lord in the splendor of his holiness" (1 Chron. 16:29).

We dedicate it to *prayer.* The psalmist says, "Lift up your hands in the sanctuary and praise the Lord" (Ps. 134:2).

We dedicate it to *praise:* "I will declare your name to my brothers; in the congregation I will praise you" (Ps. 22:22).

We dedicate it to *preaching.* Paul reminds Timothy, "Preach the Word; be prepared in season and out of season; correct, rebuke and encourage—with great patience and careful instruction" (2 Tim. 4:2).

We dedicate it to *evangelism.* Paul also charges Timothy to "do the work of an evangelist" (2 Tim. 4:5).

We dedicate it to the *development of Christian character.* We are to "grow in the grace and knowledge of our Lord and Savior Jesus Christ" (2 Peter 3:18).

We dedicate it to *God's glory.* "To him be the glory in the church and in Christ Jesus throughout all generations, for ever and ever! Amen" (Eph. 3:21).

We dedicate it in the name of Christ who bought the church of God with his own blood (Acts 20:28).

Parsonage

In Deuteronomy 20:5 God asks, "Has anyone built a new house and not dedicated it?" It is God's will that we gather to dedicate this new house for our pastor. However, we would dedicate it not as brick, mortar, glass, and lumber, but as a home.

What is a "home"? It is

A world of strife shut out—a world of love shut in.
The only spot on earth where the faults and failings
of fallen humanity
Are hidden under the mantle of charity.
The father's kingdom, the children's paradise,
the mother's world.

But a home is even more than this. A home is where tears are dried, dreams are born, and where love abides. A home, says William Cowper, is

Domestic happiness! Thou only bliss
Of Paradise that has survived the fall.

Or as Sir John Bowering says, "The happy family is but an earlier heaven."

A home is not a home unless God is an unseen resident there. Horace Bushnell says, "A house without a roof would scarcely be a more different home than a family unsheltered by God's friendship and the sense of being always rested in His providential care and guidance."

In dedicating this house we know that it will truly be a home. Our act of dedication does not end with this ceremony. It will continue as each of us blesses it with our love and prayers.

A little child walked past a house with his mother. Suddenly realizing that it was the pastor's home, he exclaimed, "God lives there!" May this ever be true of *this* parsonage!

Educational Building

A building is whatever men make of it. It can be a blight or a blessing. It can be a place of sobs or of songs. It can curse or it can cure. It can edify or it can destroy.

We are gathered today to dedicate this building. It has been built by love and sacrifice in order to enlarge the horizons of our lives.

The Christian religion is a teaching religion. It magnifies the mind as well as the spirit. This building is dedicated to education—plus. And that "plus" is religion.

Someone has said that education without religion will fill the world with clever devils. In contrast, "religious education should exalt and dignify the body and give a religious interpretation to the whole physical environment."

As we dedicate this building, we must also dedicate ourselves to its proper use. It is not an end unto itself. It is nothing more than a tool. It will not go into the community and say, "Come into my halls, learn about Jesus Christ, and be saved." But it is a place to which *we* must invite men, women and children.

Jesus tells the story of a king who prepared a marriage feast for his son. When everything was ready he sent his servants to say, ". . . everything is ready. Come . . ." (Matt. 22:4). We are those servants. Therefore, from this brief ceremony let us go with the message, "Everything is ready. Come. . . ."

General Dedication

We are assembled to dedicate this _____.
To dedicate means to devote, to offer, to consecrate.

First, *we would devote it.* To devote means to set apart for a higher end. In this sense we give it up wholly to God. By his grace and power we have received it. He gave it to us; we give it back to him. And as we give him this, we give ourselves.

Furthermore, *we would offer it.* To offer means to present something as an act of worship or sacrifice. God, who made all things, does not need our gifts. But we need to give them. In so doing we recognize God as the giver of every good and perfect gift. Our offering becomes our sacrifice. It becomes a token of a greater sacrifice, as we offer our bodies as living sacrifices to him.

Finally, *we would consecrate it.* To consecrate means to set apart for the service of God. We serve God as we serve others. As this instrument is used in the service of others it will become God's ministry through us, to the end that men shall come to know him who made heaven and earth, and through whom we may become new creations.

8

Responses to Welcomes

New Pastor

The Chinese have a saying that a journey of a thousand miles begins with one step. My first step is to welcome you to our hearts as you have opened yours to us. But the psalmist utters an even greater truth when he says, "How good and pleasant it is when brothers live together in unity" (Ps. 133:1), a unity of love, fellowship, faith, service, and purpose.

As your pastor it is not my intention to drive but to lead. I do not pose as an expert in things pertaining to the spirit; I am a sinner saved by grace. As such I shall make mistakes. I shall not always live up to your expectations. But these failures, I pray, shall be of the head, and not of the heart. I ask for your prayerful sympathy and understanding.

This task is too great for me to perform. It calls for a community of service. One of the great words in the Bible is *fellowship.* This suggests sharing mutual woes and burdens. Likewise we shall share our joy, "for we are God's fellow workers" (1 Cor. 3:9).

> Hark, the voice of Jesus calling,
> "Who will go and work today?
> Fields are white, and harvests waiting,
> Who will bear the sheaves away?"
>
> Loud and long the Master calleth,
> Rich reward He offers free;
> Who will answer, gladly, saying,
> "Here am I, send me, send me"?

> —*Daniel March*

Former Pastor

The gracious words of welcome spoken by your pastor come from his great and generous heart. We stand before you today, not as predecessor and successor, but as friends in Christ, as fellow laborers in a common cause.

By the grace of God each of us has been privileged to serve you as Christ's shepherd. Neither of us has done so in a spirit of rivalry or for self-aggrandizement. We both feed the flock of God.

The church in Corinth was troubled by divided loyalties. One member said, "I follow Paul"; another said, "I follow Apollos." With Paul I would say, "What, after all, is Apollos? And what is Paul? Only servants, through whom you came to believe—as the Lord has assigned to each his task. I planted the seed, Apollos watered it, but God made it grow. So neither he who plants nor he who waters is anything, but only God, who makes things grow. The man who plants and the man who waters have one purpose, and each will be rewarded according to his own labor" (1 Cor. 3:5–8). And that reward is from God, not from men.

So today we renew our fellowship with you, a fellowship enriched by your pastor, my friend. May the Lord, by his Holy Spirit, make us one as we look to him for his blessing.

> Brethren, we have met to worship
> And adore the Lord our God;
> Will you pray with all your power,
> While we try to preach the Word?
>
> All is vain unless the Spirit
> Of the Holy One comes down;
> Brethren, pray, and holy manna
> Will be showered all around.
>
> —George Atkins

Minister as Civic Club Speaker

Thank you, Mr. Chairman, for your heart-warming welcome.

As I come to you today, I do not come as Reverend _____; I stand before you as a man, a fellow citizen, who comes with a message from God.

When Paul and Barnabas visited Lystra, the people tried to welcome them as gods. Paul replied, "Men, why are you doing this? We too are only men, humans like you. We are bringing you good news . . ." (Acts 14:15). Some people think that there are four genders: male, female, neuter, and preachers. But preachers are people.

Jesus' favorite title for himself was "Son of Man." On the day of Pentecost, Peter began his sermon with the statement "Jesus of Nazareth was a man . . ." (Acts 2:22). It was because Jesus completely identified with man that he could be our Savior. Only as I identify with you can I hope to speak to your deepest needs.

I would remind you, however, that as a man Jesus never stooped to a level lower than the highest. Indeed, it is in him that we see the goal of true manhood. Even though I fall far short of that goal, yet by his grace I stand as his messenger. When my message is delivered, may its refrain be

> Follow with reverent steps the great example
> Of Him whose holy work was doing good;
> So shall the wide earth seem our Father's temple,
> Each loving life a psalm of gratitude.

> —*John G. Whittier*

Guest Speaker

I am honored and humbled by your words of welcome. This is especially true because of this opportunity.

One preacher asked another, "If you were going to preach just one sermon, what would it be?" Perhaps I shall preach to you only this one time. What, then, shall I preach?

Benjamin Disraeli once said, "The secret of success in life is for a man to be ready for his opportunity when it comes." This is an hour of opportunity for us. Am I ready to preach? Are you ready to listen? For both are necessary if the sermon is to achieve its intended purpose.

There is one message which surpasses all others: the story of God's redeeming love in Christ Jesus. As light passed through a prism is broken down into many colors, so God's message may be seen in many ways. May your eyes behold his beauty and your hearts perceive his grace, as together we meditate on his Word.

Guest Evangelist

Thank you, Brother Pastor, for your gracious welcome.

John Bunyan put these words into the mouth of one of his characters: "I will talk of things heavenly, or things earthly; things moral, or things evangelical; things sacred, or things profane; things past, or things to come; things foreign, or things at home; things more essential, or things circumstantial." But I am "resolved to know nothing . . . except Jesus Christ and him crucified" (1 Cor. 2:2).

We must search our hearts to do God's will. Ours is a crusade of conquest, so we must be good soldiers of Jesus Christ. Now is the time of harvest. Therefore, as laborers we must go into the field.

If a revival is to come, it must begin in churches like yours. But churches are revived only when their members experience renewed spirits and lives. When that happens, souls will be saved and lives will be reclaimed. So my prayer is

> Lord, send a revival, Lord, send a
> revival,
> Lord, send a revival, and let it begin in
> me.

*—B. B. McKinney**

Guest Speaker at a Father–Son Banquet

How can I thank you, Mr. Chairman, for your generous words of welcome?

Ben Jonson once wrote, "Greatness of name in the father oftimes overwhelms the son; they stand too near one another. The shadow kills the growth: so much, that we see the grandchild come more and oftener to be heir of the first."

But does this have to be true? Perhaps this nearness can generate bonds of unity instead of bars of separation. It is to this end that this night is dedicated.

You have honored me in inviting me to be your speaker. But you have placed upon me a great obligation. My presence tonight will be fully rewarded if I can inspire one father to say, "My son!" and one son to say, "My dad!"

Guest Speaker at a Mother–Daughter Banquet

As I look at you, two words come to mind: *beauty* and *love.* Someone has said, "Beautiful thoughts make a beautiful soul, and a beautiful soul makes a beautiful face." James Thomson once wrote, "Loveliness needs not the foreign aid of ornament, but is when unadorn'd, adorn'd the most." Martin Luther said, "Love is the image of God, and not a lifeless image, but the living essence of the divine nature which beams full of goodness."

In light of these words, this is a special moment, for beauty and love are here. Ralph Waldo Emerson said, "Tho' we travel the world over to find the beautiful, we must have it in us or find it not."

This night is one of beauty, because it is one of love. We are not here to get these virtues, but to enhance them. My prayer is "may the favor [beauty] of the Lord our God rest upon us" (Ps. 90:17), and may "the love of God" be "poured . . . into our hearts by the Holy Spirit, whom he has given us (Rom. 5:5).

Guest Speaker in Men's Brotherhood

Thank you, Mr. President, for inviting me to be with you, and for your warm words of welcome.

William Shakespeare once wrote:

> What a piece of work is man!
> How noble in reason!
> How infinite in faculties!
> In form and moving
>   how express and admirable!
> In action, how like an angel!
> In apprehension, how like a god!

If you think that this description does not fit you, perhaps it is because you do not know yourself.

We are here to understand ourselves and God's will for our lives. Ralph Waldo Emerson said, "A man is like a bit of Labrador spur, which has not luster as you turn it in your hand until you come to a particular angle; then it shows deep and beautiful colors." Seen in the light of God, you become deep and beautiful indeed.

Alexander Pope was only partially correct when he said, "The proper study of mankind is man." He should have added, "as God sees him." This truth is eloquently affirmed by Thomas Carlyle: "The older I grow—and I now stand on the brink of eternity—the more comes back to me that sentence I learned in catechism when a child, and the fuller and deeper its meaning becomes: 'What is the chief end of man? To glorify God and enjoy Him forever.' "

Guest Denominational Leader

Words are inadequate, Brother Pastor, as I try to express my joy today. But I would be untrue to my own convictions if I did not say that in your most charitable welcome, you told only half of the story.

If, as you say, I am the personification of our united endeavor, then the picture is not complete until it includes each one of you. Our denominational program is *your* work. Together we must seek to do the Lord's bidding.

In the days before electric motors furnished windpower for pipe organs, this was accomplished by hand. It seems that a certain concert organist was accustomed to accepting the applause of his audiences, with no recognition being given to the boy who

71

pumped wind into the organ. One night the organist sat before his waiting audience to play. But when he pressed upon the organ keys, nothing happened, After several unsuccessful attempts, the organist heard a sound coming from the side of the console. Looking down, he saw the boy. With an impish grin, the boy said, "Say 'we,' mister, say 'we'!"

So I would say "we," as together we do the work of the Lord.

Responses

9

Responses to Welcome of the Church Family

New Pastor

—1—

My wife and I, together with our entire family, appreciate beyond measure the gracious words of welcome spoken by the chairman of the deacons/stewards/elders, Brother _____. I know that he spoke for you. We are happy to be with you, and look forward to a ministry together for the Lord.

This day and the unfolding future are the work of the Holy Spirit. He has brought us together in ways we cannot comprehend. And the work which he has begun in us he will complete to the glory of our Lord Jesus Christ. In our planning and labors together we must be sensitive to his leadership. We should seek not merely to do our own wills, but the will of God as he reveals it to us through his Spirit.

The New Testament does not speak of church "membership" but of church "fellowship," and this "fellowship" is the work of the Holy Spirit in and among us. Paul reminds us that each Christian is the temple of the Holy Spirit. He also says that the church is the temple of the Holy Spirit. As he has led us together as pastor and people, so he blends our lives together in fellowship.

Someone has defined fellowship as two fellows in the same ship. Actually the Greek word means having all things in common, sharing. We share in both the privileges and responsibilities of the church fellowship. So as we "fellows" launch our "ship" today, the effectiveness and pleasure of the voyage depend upon sharing each other's blessings and burdens.

Today we pledge to you our best, and we expect from you your best. The Lord's business deserves no less. May God bless us all as we become one in Christ, united in purpose and devotion to him who has called us to be fellow laborers in his vineyard.

—2—

My family joins me in expressing our gratitude for the gracious welcome you have given to us. Our hearts go out to meet yours in Christian love. And as time passes, that mutual love will grow into a fellowship which exceeds all other human relationships.

Speaking of himself and Apollos, Paul writes in 1 Corinthians 3:9, "For we are God's fellow workers." His emphasis is on *belonging to God.* So *we* are fellow workers because we belong to God.

This truth is equally applicable to us today. We belong to God. We are his children—both pastor and people. And by his grace we are *fellow workers.* This does not mean that God is on one side of the yoke and we are on the other. It means that as God's children we help each other in doing his work. He strengthens and guides us in the task, but his power and purpose depend upon our cooperative endeavor in his name.

On occasion I have heard people speak of "hiring a preacher." But, beloved, you cannot *hire* someone else to do your work for the Lord. I cannot do yours and you cannot do mine. Each person has his or her own work to do. Nehemiah 4:15 describes building the walls of Jerusalem in terms of "each to his own work." In one of his parables Jesus uses the phrase "each with his assigned task" (Mark 13:34). In Nehemiah 4:6 we find the vivid description, "So we rebuilt the wall . . . for the people worked with all their heart." This is the formula by which we shall accomplish the purpose for which the Lord has brought us together.

We shall do well to heed this commonsense statement from an anonymous writer: "The fellow who is pulling the oars usually hasn't time to rock the boat." So let us put our hands to the oars. Through cooperative endeavor we shall bring the Lord's ship— our church—into its intended port of call. To this end we pledge ourselves today. If you join me in this pledge, may we stand with clasped hands, bowed heads, and united hearts as we are led in a prayer of dedication by Brother _____, chairman of our deacons/elders/stewards.

—3—

With a grateful heart I am delighted to respond to the welcome you have given to me and my family today.

First of all, let me say that I have not come to take

the place of my predecessor, but to make a place of my own in your hearts. Do not be afraid to tell me of your love for him and his family. Frankly, if you did not love them, we would be afraid of you; the fact that you love them shows your capacity to love us.

A pastor was to begin his new charge. Wishing to coordinate the music with the new pastor's first sermon, the music director asked about the sermon topic. Jokingly the pastor replied, "Well, I always try to have my sermon fit the occasion. Since it will be my first sermon following a long line of previous pastors, I think I will preach on John 10:8: 'All who ever came before me were thieves and robbers.' " The music leader exclaimed, "Over my dead body you will!"

My predecessors were capable and honorable men. Therefore, I shall not seek to destroy what they did, but to build on it. In time I shall present other programs which I trust will enhance theirs; I welcome your suggestions as to what these programs will be.

So in the spirit of mutual affection I want to preach to you on the words of Paul found in 1 Corinthians 3:6: "I planted the seed, Apollos watered it, but God made it grow." I do not do violence to Paul's meaning if I paraphrase his words as follows: "Others have planted, I shall water; but it is God who causes growth."

—4—

My words are inadequate in response to your gracious welcome. Of course, we are happy to be here, or we would be somewhere else. I am sure that this is God's will, or I would seek it elsewhere.

Instead of turning this into a mutual admiration society, let us turn to the Bible for words which describe the relationship we have formed in the Lord. I wish to choose two passages, both of which come from the apostle Paul.

In Acts 20:28 Paul is addressing the elders of the church in Ephesus. He says: "Keep watch over yourselves and all the flock of which the Holy Spirit has made you overseers [bishops]. Be shepherds of the church of God, which he bought with his own blood."

Keep in mind that Paul is speaking to *elders.* He calls them *overseers,* or bishops. And he tells them to be like shepherds or *pastors* in the church of God. An elder offers wise counsel, a bishop is an overseer who makes sure that others do their work properly, and a pastor is one who feeds and cares for the flock.

I will attempt to fill this threefold office among you: to counsel you in your problems and sorrows, to lead you in your work for the Lord, and to feed and care for you as a shepherd does his flock. Needless to say, this is a demanding role. But with the Lord's help I shall try to measure up to its demands.

The other passage is found in Ephesians 4:11–13 (KJV): "And he [Christ] gave some, apostles; and some, prophets; and some, evangelists; and some, pastors and teachers; For the perfecting [equipping] of the saints, for the work of the ministry, for the edifying of the body of Christ: Till we all come in [into] the unity of the faith, and of the knowledge [full knowledge] of the Son of God, unto a perfect [mature] man, unto the measure of the stature of the fulness of Christ."

Unfortunately, the punctuation of these verses in the King James Version is misleading. Verse 13 seems to describe the work of "pastors and teachers": to perfect the saints, to do the work of the ministry, and to build up the body of Christ. The Greek text uses no punctuation marks except the question mark. The punctuation was added by translators as they interpreted the meaning. We, therefore, will do well to remove the punctuation in order to discern Paul's meaning. The text then reads, "And he gave some . . . pastors and teachers [referring to one office] for the equipping of the saints for the work of the ministry for the purpose of building up the body of Christ."

A pastor is to equip the people of Christ to enable them to be his servants for the purpose of building up his body. The result will be a unity of faith involving a full knowledge of the Son of God—mature Christians—so that the body of Christ will be in proper proportion to its head.

Now this does not mean that the pastor is simply to be a boss telling others what to do and how to do it. He is a fellow worker, setting an example for others to follow. He must not say, "Here is what you must do, so get on with your work." Rather he says, "Here is our task. Let's get on with it together!"

It is in this spirit that we come to you. May this be the spirit which characterizes our relationship!

—5—

Thank you, Brother _____, for your warm words of welcome spoken on behalf of the church.

Mingled with our joy is a sense of fear. A specialist in visitation-evangelism once instructed a group of people before sending them out on their first assignment: "When you knock on the first door, you will be scared to death. And I hope you are. Otherwise, you will be unable to do your best." This same principle applies to me and my family.

80

Two reasons for this are the enormity of the task and the greatness of the opportunity. When Paul came to Corinth, he was faced with an awesome task. He writes: "I came to you in weakness and fear, and with much trembling" (1 Cor. 2:3).

I suppose that this sense of fear comes from being in a strange place with new people. We are not afraid of you; you are our comfort and strength. At the same time, however, there lies before us the task of getting acquainted. It is always the same with any new pastor and his church. But whereas you have only a few faces and names to remember, mine and those of my family, I have many. But in time we shall be able to put faces and names together.

During the course of a year an evangelist went into many churches and met thousands of new people. Whenever he went to the national convention of his denomination some of these people would invariably come to him and say, "I am sure you do not know my name." Of course, in most cases he did not. Rather than embarrass them, however, he would reply, "Why, my friend, I'll know you in heaven!"

While we will know your names in heaven, we also want to know them now. So do not ask if we know your name. Tell us, and soon we will be telling it to you! God bless you, dear friends. We are overjoyed to be here and look forward to working with you!

New Pastor to the Church Staff

—1—

We sometimes hear a statement described as "trite." But a statement is usually trite only because it is true. Through frequent use it comes to be known as trite.

At the risk of sounding trite, then, I want to say in response to your welcome that I appreciate it more than words can express. Your generous attitude toward me warms my heart and challenges my spirit. For I realize that the effectiveness of my ministry here depends to a great degree on you. And I want to pledge my best to you in our mutual ministry in and through this church.

When the church committee talked to me about coming here as pastor, they spoke highly of your ability and dedication. Yet they also gave me the opportunity to provide whatever staff I wished. I said that I wanted the present staff to remain because we could and would work together. Today my decision has been confirmed.

I believe that the Lord calls all his servants, not simply the pastor. Our Lord set the pattern for church staffs when he chose others to be with him, so to extend his own ministry. The apostle Paul often referred to those who labored with him in the gospel. So we are following a worthy precedent as we begin our service together.

Someone has said that you can employ men and hired hands to work *for* you, but you must win their hearts if they are to work *with* you. I do not regard you as hired hands. But I *do* know that our hearts must be united if we are to work together.

My position calls for me to be the leader of the staff. Yet while I am your *boss*, in a deeper sense I am your *pastor;* I prefer that our relationship be based on the latter rather than the former. For this to be true we must share mutual love and loyalty. I shall give both, and I know that you will do the same. This does not mean that we shall not have our problems;

this is part of any human relationship. But we shall resolve them in frank, open discussion.

If the time should come when we hold two different positions and one must prevail, it should be mine. However, I do not anticipate that this will happen often. For I have learned that there are usually three sides to every question: yours, mine, and the right one. Somewhere between yours and mine is the right one, and with God's grace we shall find it.

As I said a moment ago, I do not regard you as hired hands. Each of you is a specialist in your own field. This is true whether you are a building custodian, secretary, or minister in some phase of our work. As far as I am concerned, each will have a free hand within the framework of our staff structure. The church does not *buy* so many hours of your time and pounds of your energy. It asks you to bring to your position imagination, ingenuity, vision, and effort toward making the entire church program more effective.

Now to you who occupy positions of leadership in various areas, I shall delegate not only responsibility but authority. Each of you has your own staff within a staff. The people on your staff should be responsible to you alone. As pastor I will not correct them. I will deal with you, leaving you free and responsible to deal with them. This will make for good, orderly staff relationships.

We shall all operate within the established policies of the church. If you and I agree on a certain program and, in implementing it, you run into difficulties, you will find me by your side. But at all times let us move together. Periodic staff meetings will enable us to do this. It is my wish that each member of the staff be informed about the entire church program; information is necessary for intelligent cooperation.

If two of you disagree, get together and talk about it. If that fails, then talk with your staff supervisor. Do not discuss your problems with the staff or the larger church family. The more people who know about a problem, the more difficult it is to solve. If you have a problem that concerns me, come to me with it. We will resolve it in Christian love. Happy staff relations will be reflected throughout the church; unfortunately, the opposite is also true.

Let us remember that while we work for the Lord, we also work for and with the church family. So let us strive to be Christlike in all of our relationships. With regard to our interstaff and other church relationships, let us show Christian courtesy. In closing, let me share some words from an unknown author:

> I am a little thing with a big meaning.
> I help everyone.
> I unlock doors, open hearts, banish prejudice;
> I create friendship and good will.
> I inspire respect and admiration.
> I violate no law.
> I cost nothing. Many have praised me; none have condemned me.
> I am pleasing to those of high and low degree.
> I am useful every moment.
> I am courtesy!

—2—

Thanks for your enthusiastic words of welcome and your pledge of cooperation. If I am to have a fruitful ministry here, I need you far more than you need me.

Some years ago a pastor wrote a book entitled *Moses' Mighty Men,* a character study of the men who helped Moses in his ministry. The author asserted that it takes three things to make a great man: he must be endowed with the capacity for greatness; he must be in a historical environment which calls forth his greatness; he must be surrounded by lesser greats who contribute to his own greatness.

I do not consider myself endowed with the capacity for greatness. But the capacities which I have, I have dedicated to the Lord. Neither do I consider you as "lesser greats." But there *is* an analogy in degree.

Members of this church have expressed their confidence in me; I possess certain qualities which they want in a pastor. So I find myself placed in an environment which calls on those abilities.

I want to be the best pastor I can possibly be. However, I realize that for this to be true, you must surround me and strengthen me with your abilities. It is to this end that I would blend my life with yours, for without your help I shall be unable to measure up to the trust placed in me.

I do not need to remind you that we are in this work together. If we succeed, it will be *together.* If we fail, it will be *together.* So let us erase the word *failure* from the dictionaries of our lives and rejoice in the success of our Lord's work—a success which *together* we will lay at his feet as testimony to his grace.

Church Staff to a New Pastor

—1—

Our hearts are warmed beyond measure by the words you have spoken to us. During the time our

85

church was seeking a pastor, we prayed earnestly for the committee charged with this tremendous responsibility. We feel that our prayers have been answered.

I have been chosen by the church staff as their spokesman on this occasion. We welcome you as one. We are ready to follow your leadership. Your open-mindedness toward us and the work encourages us to feel that under your guidance we can make our best contribution to this church.

We have always thought of ourselves as a family. While in our eager enthusiasm for the work we may have our differences of opinion, they have never made a difference in our hearts. We are happy that we can add your heart to ours.

We pledge our loyalty to you as our leader. Someone has said that "a leader sees three things: what ought to be done, what can be done, and how to do it." We believe that we have such a leader in you. As you exercise your leadership we will follow. In so doing we give you not only our hands but also our hearts, not only our might but also our minds, and not only our labor but also our love.

So, pastor, mark out the path we shall follow, and you will find us by your side.

—2—

I have not been officially designated to respond to your gracious words to us in this first staff meeting with you. But, like Simon Peter, I feel that I can speak for the group since I know their hearts.

Frankly, we have all been anxious while the church was seeking a new pastor. We were not fearful, but wondered what kind of person he would be. And now your words have put us at ease.

One of the highest compliments Dr. George W. Truett could pay to a person was to say, "He is our kind of folks." And that is our opinion about you. You are our kind of folks, and we look forward to working with you.

New Pastor to the Deacons

—1—

Brother Chairman, I am overjoyed to receive your words spoken on behalf of the deacons. They echo the spirit of the entire congregation which has so warmly received me and my family. Though we have been here only a few days, we already feel at home among you.

Like begets like; your love for us enhances the love we have for you. Eugenia Price once wrote, "We love according to the way people treat us." James Russell Lowell also reminds us that "they who love are but one step from heaven." Because of this we are going to share a special relationship as pastor and people.

The New Testament mentions only pastors and deacons as ordained offices in the church. For that reason ours is a peculiar and most intimate relationship. We shall work together more closely than any other people in the church.

The New Testament does not clearly state the origin of the office of deacon. The Greek word so translated means *servant*. Usually the institution of the office is identified in Acts 6. The burden of spiritual and material ministry to the church in Jerusalem became too demanding for the apostles to bear alone.

At their suggestion the church selected "seven men ... full of the [Holy] Spirit and wisdom" who were set apart to care for the physical needs of the widows. This allowed the apostles to spend more time in prayer and in the ministry of the Word.

However, the ministry of deacons is not limited to material concerns. This is exemplified by Stephen and Philip. Stephen was the first Christian martyr to die because of his powerful preaching of the gospel. Philip became known as an evangelist due to his effectiveness and zeal in this work. Both Jesus and Paul on occasion referred to themselves as deacons or ministers. Thus we see that there is overlap in the positions of pastor and deacon. Each of us will complement the other as we join our unique abilities and use them in the Lord's service.

One further thing needs to be said. Acts 6:7 describes the results following the selection of the first deacons: "So the word of God spread. The number of disciples in Jerusalem increased rapidly, and a large number of priests [the most difficult to reach with the gospel] became obedient to the faith."

When a pastor and deacons work together, the work of the Lord will prosper. This church will rise no higher or progress no further than the vision and leadership of its pastor and deacons. It is to this end that we join hearts and hands to pursue the work to which we have been called.

—2—

Thank you so much, Brother Chairman, for your kind words which reflect your spirit, one which is necessary if the Lord's work is to prosper in our church.

I need not remind you that the church has not elected you to your high offices in order to honor you. The church has chosen you because through your spirit and faithfulness you have proved yourselves honorable. The honor related to your position is how you honor it. And you do this by proving faithful to the trust that the church has placed in you.

The church could not afford to buy the knowledge and skills which you possess. Yet you give them freely for a single reason—your love for Christ and his church.

Several years ago a church borrowed a large sum of money from a bank in order to erect a new building. The bank officer asked for the names of those on the church's finance committee. When the officer looked at it, he said, "Your finance committee is stronger than ours." All of them were deacons.

As your pastor I shall rely heavily on your counsel and guidance, not in business matters alone but also in matters concerning the entire life of our church. It is only by working together that we can prove worthy of our respective responsibilities.

Pray for me as I will be praying for you. A pastor can receive both spiritual and physical strength from his deacons. Once each week a certain deacon would drop by his pastor's office, and say, "Pastor, I do not want a thing. I just dropped by to pray with you." My door will always be open to you, for whatever purpose you may come: to counsel, to criticize, but especially for you to come by and pray with me.

In the future I will be asking you for many things pertaining to the life and ministry of our church. But for the moment I ask that you join me in a prayer of dedication, using the words of an unknown poet.

Laid on Thine altar, O my Lord, Divine,
  Accept my gift this day, for Jesus' sake.
I have no jewels to adorn thy shrine,
  No world-famed sacrifice to make;
And here I bring within my trembling hands
  This will of mine, a thing that seemeth small,
Yet Thou alone canst understand
  How when I yield Thee this, I yield Thee all.

New Pastor to the Women's Missionary Union

Thank you, Madam Director/President/Chairman, for your wonderful words of welcome. Being here is a privilege my wife and I have been looking forward to.

Women play a prominent role in Luke's account of Jesus' life and ministry. In Luke 8:2–3, he mentions certain women who "were helping to support them out of their own means." Jesus had ministered to them, and they ministered to him in turn. One scholar calls this little group the first women's missionary society.

Not only do you serve our church in various ways, but you are also its missionary conscience. Through study, prayer, and giving, you undergird the missionary work of our denomination throughout the world. A church which lives only for itself is a dying church. A missionary church is a living church. Our church is alive, largely due to you.

As your pastor, I want to undergird your work as you do mine. For, after all, it is the same work—that of the Lord. I welcome not only your service, but also your suggestions. A wise man once said, "Frequently, when doubtful how to act in matters of importance,

I have received more useful advice from women than from men. Women have the understanding of the heart, which is better than that of the head." I know that this is true in my home, and it is also true in the church. In Christian love my wife and I join hands and hearts with you in the work of the Lord.

New Pastor to the Men of the Church

May God bless you, Brother, for your enthusiastic words of welcome. This is a time of special joy for me.

In God's providence there are aspects of his work that only men can fill. This is not to discount the faithful service of women. It is rather to magnify the place of men in spiritual endeavor. I have never known a church to reach its full potential without a large group of dedicated men.

Goethe once wrote, "One cannot always be a hero, but he can always be a man." The supreme pattern of manhood is demonstrated in Jesus Christ. In his strength tempered by tenderness, he received the following of women; in his strength geared to purpose, he challenged the loyalty of men.

I do not come to you as a pompous know-it-all with ready-made answers for the problems of our church and community. Neither do I come to impose my will on you. You know the needs of our church far better than I do. So like our Savior, I am among you as one who serves. I need and welcome your counsel, and I am sure that I shall receive your cooperation. *Together* we shall chart the course and supply the power for the way in which our church should go.

Let these words from Gerhard Friedrich challenge you:

> We read quite clearly the blueprint of our souls, and yet fail miserably to translate its perfect proportions into the reality of our lives. Spiritual complacency is the main sin of mankind. Have we ever been fervently and religiously grateful for every breath we draw? Have we ever seriously tried to dig up a piece of this old earth and to plant it anew? Choose whatever language you wish and whatever terms you like best; make your conclusions as broad and as unorthodox as you please; even in this streamlined, superbombed age, godly men are needed!

New Pastor to the Young People

Knowing young people as I do, I am sure that you do not want me to make a long speech. Frankly, I do not like to listen to long speeches either. However, I simply must express my thanks for your welcome to this youth fellowship. I trust that from now on you will consider me as one of your group.

A few years separate us in age. But age is a state of mind as well as a total number of years. I have known some people who were old at twenty, and others who were young at seventy.

A mother took her teenaged daughter to Florida for the winter. The girl was hoping to have a great time in Miami. Imagine her surprise when she learned that they were going to St. Petersburg, the retirement capital of Florida! Since she saw no one but old people, she became a recluse, refusing to leave her hotel room. Her mother was worried about her.

One day she said to her daughter, "Honey, let's go down to the park and hear Moses' band." The daughter exclaimed, "Don't tell me *that* old man is still living, and has a band here in St. Petersburg!"

Well, I am not as old as Moses or as young as you are. But I look forward to having fun with you as together we serve the Lord. Let me be your pastor in the deepest sense of the word. When you have a church get-together, include me in it. When you have problems, let me help you with them. Okay? Okay!

10

Responses on Various Church Occasions

Guest Pulpit Supply

—1—

Thank you, Brother _____, for your gracious words of welcome to your church today. As you know, I have been your guest minister many times in the past. Because of the warm spirit I always find here, I have been looking forward to this visit.

Your pastor, my friend through the years, is one of the noblest of God's servants. You are fortunate to have him as your pastor. Furthermore, you are gracious to share him with others from time to time. He will return to you next Lord's day refreshed for his work here because of his experience.

As a pastor, I have always regarded my own church as my primary ministry. However, I also feel that I am serving my church by serving other churches in our denomination. It is because your pastor is capable that he is asked to serve in other places. So be thankful that while other churches are blessed by his ministry now and then, you are blessed regularly.

I cannot hope to take his place here today, but with the Lord's help I will seek to be his spokesman for this hour. Will you pray for me as I preach the Word?

—2—

Brother _____, I can never tell you how much I appreciate your kind words of welcome.

I am sure that many of you would be happy if your pastor was never gone. And I can understand why. When I was in the pastorate, I had a deacon who loved me dearly. When I would return after being gone, he would say, "Well, you've been gone again!" One day I replied "You know something? You remind me of the man who wanted his wife at home on two occasions—when he was there and when he wasn't there."

But, you know, any man who is capable of being the pastor of this church will always be in demand elsewhere. Our denomination must have ministerial leadership, and pastors like yours must supply it. Thus he is serving this church, whether he is in this pulpit or in another. I know that you share this conviction with me. And that is why today we shall rejoice in the Lord who is both here with us and with your pastor as he serves elsewhere.

God bless you for who and what you are! And now for my text.

Denominational Leader

Thank you, pastor, for your words of welcome and for permitting me to be here today. As you said, I am the executive secretary of the _____ Board. One of my preacher friends refers to me as a "board head." But "board head" or not, I hope for the next few minutes to be a preacher of the gospel. And now for my text.

Executive Secretary of the Home (Foreign) Mission Board

—1—

Brother Pastor, it is a great privilege to preach here today. Your generous words of welcome enhance my joy.

You introduced me as a missionary. I am; I represent that vast army of men and women who stand in the breach for our Lord in places where his name is rarely heard.

However, you are also missionaries—those who are sent. Someone once defined a true missionary as "God's man in God's place, doing God's work in God's way for God's glory." At the local church level we call this task *evangelism.* Elsewhere we call it *missions.* But the task is one and the same—declaring the gospel to those who are lost wherever they may be.

Someone else reminds us that "visions without work are visionary; work without vision is mercenary; together they are missionary." Therefore, my purpose today is to challenge you: Where you can witness for Christ, you should; where you cannot go, you should give to send others. If I can succeed in leading you to do these two things, then my coming to you will not have been in vain.

Madame Director/President, I am grateful for your words of welcome.

As we enjoy this delicious meal in comfortable surroundings, I am reminded of the story of an African pastor. To missionaries going on furlough, he said, "Tell our friends in America that we do not have refrigerators and other modern conveniences. Tell them that we even get along without automobiles. But tell them we cannot do without the gospel of the Son of God."

There are some who would have us believe that world mission outreach has failed. However, the problem is a lack of mission outreach.

A French trader saw a New Hebrides chief reading the Bible. He said, "Bah! Why are you reading the Bible? I suppose the missionaries have gotten hold of you, you poor fool. Throw it away! The Bible never did anyone any good." Calmly the chief replied, "If it weren't for this Bible, you'd be in my kettle now." So it is simply a question as to what one means by success. To this infidel trader, mission outreach was successful indeed.

Mission outreach is what the church is all about. Paul, in Ephesians 3:10–11, says that God's eternal purpose of redemption in Christ is to be made known through the church. Foreign missions will be no stronger or more effective than missions here at home. Worldwide enterprises demand a strong home base of operations. So my plea is not simply for foreign missions, but for all missions, beginning right here in this church.

The great theologian Augustus H. Strong once

asked some probing questions I would like to ask you:

What are the churches for but to make missionaries?
What is education for but to train them?
What is commerce for but to carry them?
What is money for but to send them?
What is life itself for but to fulfill the purpose of Missions!
the enthroning of Jesus
in the hearts of men?

Convert from the Mission Field

Madame Director/President, I thank you for your words of welcome. I hope some day to say the same things to you in my country.

You have asked me to tell you why I believe in missions. My very presence here speaks more to that point than I can say in words. I believe in missions because of what missions have done for me and many of my people. Unless you had lived with us before the missionaries came, you cannot possibly appreciate what the gospel has done for us.

I am of a different race and nationality than you. My language is different. My clothes are different. My way of life is different from yours. But I have the same sins that you have. I have the same spiritual needs that you have. Because of the gospel we are one in our Lord Jesus Christ. So, you see, I believe in missions. But I want to say something to you about why *you* should believe in missions using the words of Charles M. Sheldon:

Because the greatest mission ever known was when God sent His

only begotten Son into the world to save it.

Because the world will never be brought to Christ until men bring

Christ to the world.

Because Jesus Himself taught us that missions was the only way

to make disciples.

Because I am a disobedient lover of Jesus if I do not obey His

command when He said . . . "Go."

Because if salvation means everything to me, I cannot be happy

unless I share it with others.

Because a Christian who does not believe in missions always gets

narrow and loses his world vision.

Because the missionary is the greatest hope of the world in its

present historical crises.

My brothers and sisters in Christ, I thank you!

Guest Evangelist

Brother Pastor and Christian friends, I thank God for each one of you and the hearty welcome you have expressed to me today. Since receiving your invitation, I have made this a matter of personal prayer.

There are many satisfying rewards in being an evangelist. But there is also a price to be paid. Part of that price is missing the abiding fellowship enjoyed by a pastor and his flock. But one reward is the opportunity to share with many churches in the quest for souls. Dwight L. Moody requested only one monument for himself after death—a saved sinner telling about salvation in Jesus Christ. I could ask for no better monument for myself.

In the great grain belt of our nation, harvest crews begin in the south and sweep north with the ripening of the grain. Without the previous work done by others, the harvest would be fruitless; and when the grain is ripe, it must be reaped or the harvest is lost. Revival meetings are times of harvest. Along with your pastor you have sown the seed and tilled the soil. Now the harvest is ripe for reaping.

Unfortunately, we have been accustomed to think of revivals only in terms of winning the lost. But the very word *revival* points to the church itself. You cannot *re*vive someone who has not been "vived." So we Christians must be *re-vived.* That will result in our renewed effort to witness to the lost for Christ. Winning the lost is not the *means* of revival but the *fruit* of it.

So I challenge you to join me in making ourselves available to the Holy Spirit who would lead us in our search for those who need to come to Christ. It is to this end that my first sermon in this series is devoted. Turn with me in your Bibles to 2 Chronicles 7:14 where God gives his formula for a revival: "If my people, who are called by my name, will humble themselves and pray and seek my face and turn from their wicked ways, then will I hear from heaven and will forgive their sin and will heal their land."

Former Pastor

My dear friends, how can I ever thank you adequately for your kind invitation to visit again and to have warm fellowship with you? It is good to be here.

A young Methodist pastor was serving in his first church. After the first year, there was an increase in attendance, membership, and missionary giving. After finishing the church's annual report, he proudly showed it to the chairman of stewards. After looking it over, the chairman said, "This is fine, pastor! With a report like this, maybe the bishop will send us a *good* preacher next year."

Well, the Lord sent one to you. No one could be happier than I am. Your pastor is my friend. So our mutual love for him is an added tie between us.

Now I shall preach for the Lord. My text is found in 2 Corinthians 4:5: "For we do not preach ourselves, but Jesus Christ as Lord, and ourselves as your servants for Jesus' sake."

Pastor Emeritus

My dear pastor, you have been most gracious in your words of welcome. And note that I said *"My* dear pastor." For you *are* my pastor.

I have not had a pastor for many years. So now it seems that the good Lord is making it up to me by giving me a pastor like you. Come to think about it, you also do not have a pastor. So let me be your pastor while I try to be the best member I can be. My wife and I want to help you, your family, and the church in any way we can. We have resolved that even if we cannot help you, we certainly will do nothing to harm you.

You noted that the church has made me "pastor emeritus." A friend of mine reminded me recently that Dr. Elton Trueblood, noting that he had been made "professor emeritus," said that *emeritus* comes from two Latin words: *e* meaning "out," and *meritus* meaning "deserves to be."

Though that is true, I take *emeritus* to mean "out of merit." If I merit this honor in any sense, it is because of the many years I served here as pastor. And I shall show my appreciation by trying to act in such fashion that the church will have no reason to regret its action.

Who can measure the capacity of the human heart? We are capable of so many kinds of love. For instance, the fact that you love our pastor and his family does not mean that you love me and my family any less. In fact, your lives are the richer because you have found room for all of us. And we respond in kind.

In writing to the Corinthians Paul says "our heart is enlarged" (2 Cor. 6:11, KJV)—not enlarged in the sense of suffering from a physical defect, but in the sense of having attained spiritual growth and perfection. "Our heart is enlarged"; there is a love in it great enough to include all of you.

This is why I have chosen these words for the text of our sermon this morning. I know that you will pray for me as I preach the Word.

Retired Pastor

Brother _____, I am grateful for your words of welcome as I preach in the absence of your pastor.

102

We will all be praying for him as I know he is praying for us.

I am a retired pastor. Many attempts have been made to describe what it means to be retired. Someone has defined retirement from the wife's standpoint: She has twice as much husband and half as much income. Perhaps Dennis the Menace came close. His pal Joey asked, "What did Mr. Wilson mean when he said that he is retired?" Dennis said, "I don't know. I guess it means that he was tired yesterday and he's tired again today."

Two people have tried to describe retirement in poetry. One poet writes:

> I can get along with my arthritis,
> My dentures fit me fine.
> I can see through my bifocals,
> But I sure do miss my mind.

Another says:

> I get up each morning—dust off my wits,
> Pick up the paper and read the Obits;
> If my name is missing, I know I'm not dead,
> So I eat a good breakfast and go back to bed.

But, you know, these lines don't describe me. My health is good, and I am busier than I have ever been before. I have not *retired* but *retreaded* for a different and broader ministry. I have retired from the pastorate but not from the ministry. I will not do so until the Lord who called me says, "It is enough."

I could spend the time allotted to me this hour talking about the past. But why do that when your interest and mine is in the future? Charles F. Kettering said, "My interest is in the future because I am going to spend the rest of my life there." We have lived in the past, we live in the present, and on tiptoe we anticipate the future. So for my text this morning I have chosen 1 Timothy 1:17 which is about the eternal: "Now to the King eternal, immortal, invisible, the only God, be honor and glory for ever and ever. Amen."

Public Official at a Church Dinner

—1—

Mr. President, as your governor/mayor/city councilman/police chief/fire chief, I am invited to speak to many groups. But I can assure you that none gives me greater pleasure than this one.

I come not simply as a public official but as an ally in the work of making our city a better place to live. The same God who brought the church into being also ordained the institution of government.

President George Washington once said, "While just government protects all in their religious rites, true religion affords government its surest support." A community is no better than the character of its citizens, and producing righteous character is the primary purpose of the church.

A neighborhood in one of our major cities was infested with crime. Despite all that the government did, the crime wave continued unabated. One day a preacher came to the community and started a small Sunday school; it eventually became a church. It was not long until the policemen in the area noted a decided decrease in crime. Today that neighborhood is one of the most law-abiding areas in that city.

As you do your job better it makes mine easier. Therefore, I wish to talk to you about how we can help each other in our mutual task.

—2—

Thank you, pastor, for your gracious welcome. However, as you know, I am not here as a public official to make a speech but simply as one of your flock.

But come to think about, it, I do want to say *something*. My speech is short and to the point. Someone once noted that there are thirty-five million laws but none of them improve on the Ten Commandments.

Minister of Another Denomination

—1—

My fellow pastor, you warm my heart and challenge my spirit by your generous introduction. In fact you put me on the spot as I try to show that my heart is as large as yours. The fact that you invited me to speak and that I am here is a demonstration of what Paul means when he speaks of Christians "[making] every effort to keep the unity of the Spirit through the bond of peace" (Eph. 4:3).

I recognize as you do that as different denominations we have and cherish our own beliefs and practices. However, we share a mutual faith in and a love for Christ. Though I am not a Methodist, I can say with John Wesley, "If your heart be as my heart, give me your hand." Though I am not a Baptist, I can say "amen" to the words spoken by the great English Baptist preacher John Clifford at the founding session of the Baptist World Alliance in London in 1905. Referring to their love for all Christians everywhere, he said, "We were Christians before we were Baptists." This applies to any group by whatever name they may be called.

In this spirit will all of you pray for me as I speak on Paul's words found in Ephesians 4:7? "But to each one of us grace has been given as Christ apportioned it."

—2—

Thank you, Brother Pastor, for your gracious introduction. Realizing that I am from a different denomination, I want to relate a story which leads into my message.

Before the days of television, a Baptist minister turned on his radio one Sunday afternoon. When the radio had warmed up, he heard a man preaching an evangelistic sermon. After listening for a few minutes he said to himself, "I don't know who he is, but he must be a Baptist." A little later he said again, "Yes, he is a Baptist all right." So he settled back and enjoyed this *Baptist* sermon. Imagine his surprise when, after the sermon was finished, the announcer said, "You have been listening to Father [later Bishop] Fulton J. Sheen, preaching on 'The Catholic Hour.' "

Sheen was not preaching dogma. He was simply preaching the gospel of Christ. And that is what I want to do as we turn our thoughts to Paul's words in Philippians 1:18: ". . . Christ is preached. And because of this I rejoice."

Minister of Another Race (Nationality)

—1—

My dear Christian friends, I am among you in one sense as a stranger, but in the deepest sense I am with you as a Christian brother. Though we are of different races/nationalities we are children of our heavenly Father, and joint heirs with Christ our elder brother.

The apostle Paul had the map of the world tattooed within his heart. In Galatians 3:28 he writes, "There is neither Jew nor Greek, slave nor free, male nor female, for you are all one in Christ Jesus." He covers the gamut of human experience: race, religion, economic condition, sex. All external differences are removed in Christ.

It is fitting, therefore, that I should borrow other words from Paul as the basis for my remarks today. They are found in Ephesians 2:14–15. Speaking of Jews and Gentiles who had become Christians he says, "For he himself is our peace, who has made the two one and has destroyed the barrier, the dividing wall of hostility . . . to create in himself one new man out of the two, thus making peace."

If we reduce this to a mathematical equation, it reads as follows: One Jew plus one Gentile plus Christ equals two Christian brothers. Or, one white man plus one black man plus Christ equals two Christian brothers. Or, one American plus one Russian plus Christ equals two Christian brothers. Use any combination, and the answer is always the same.

As someone has said, in Christ God is making a new order of mankind. He is making the people of God. This is the theme of my message.

Brother Pastor, I thank you for your kind and generous words. I can understand your language even though I do not speak it too well. But I want to speak a language which all of us can understand.

In 1965, Dr. William R. Tolbert, Jr., president of Liberia, was elected president of the Baptist World Alliance. When a news reporter learned that Tolbert spoke only English, he asked the president how he would communicate with people of different languages throughout the world. Tolbert replied, "I will speak the language of love."

That is the language I will speak today. Even if you have difficulty understanding my English, I know that you will understand my love.

Guest Speaker at a Mother–Daughter Banquet

Dear friends, I am grateful for your most generous words of welcome. But most of all I am happy that you have asked me to be with you tonight.

What can be more wonderful than mothers and daughters sharing such warm fellowship! There is a bond between mothers and daughters unlike any other in the world. This is not to say that there is not love between mothers and sons. But something extra has been added to mother–daughter love. What it is I do not know. Maybe it is the sameness of sex, or that peculiar sensitivity of women. However, I have an idea that it is a motherly instinct.

There is a silent understanding, call it communion if you will, which binds together the tender, sensitive love of which both mother and daughter are capable. In her tender years, a daughter naturally looks to her mother for care and guidance. And when a mother grows old, she looks to her grown daughter for love, care, and understanding. Thus the cycle of life is complete. An unnamed poet has put it in words far more beautiful than mine:

As once you stroked my thin and silver hair
  So I stroke yours now at the set of sun.
I watch your tottering mind, its day's work done,
  As once you watched with forward-looking care
My tottering feet. I love you as I should.
  Stay with me; lean on me; I'll make no sigh.
I was your child, and now time makes you mine.
  Stay with me yet a while at home, and do me good.

Guest Speaker at a Father – Son Banquet

I can think of no more wonderful occasion than when fathers and sons sit down not only to eat but to share fellowship together. We hear a lot about the "generation gap." But no such gap is evident in the heart-to-heart relationship I see here tonight.

I have never known a man who did not hope that someday he would have a son. A man somehow wants more than his family name to live on in his son. In a special way he hopes that something of himself will live on as well. A father must pass something on to his son that is worthwhile.

A boy may not always understand his father. But time has a way of nurturing in him a growing appreciation for the manly virtues he has seen in his father.

This thought is expressed in a poem by an unknown author, "My Dad."

> He couldn't speak before a crowd;
>   He couldn't teach a class;
> But when he came to Sunday school
>   He brought the folks en masse.
>
> He couldn't sing to save his life,
>   In public couldn't pray;
> But always his jalopy was just
>   Crammed on each Lord's Day.
>
> And although he couldn't sing,
>   Nor teach, nor lead in prayer,
> He listened well, he had a smile,
>   And he was always there
>
> With all the others whom he brought
>   Who lived both far and near—
> And God's work prospered, for
>   I had a consecrated dad.

Guest Speaker at a Stewardship Banquet

—1—

Brother Pastor—or should I say "Brother Shepherd"?—I thank you for your kind words of introduction.

Someone has said that a shepherd's job is to find, fold, feed, and fleece the sheep. You have found, folded, and fed them. Now it is my job to help you fleece them.

Fleecing is easier on the sheep than it is on the shepherd, just as punishing a child is less traumatic for the child than it is for his parents. As a father was spanking his little boy, he said, "Son, this hurts me as much as it does you." The boy replied, "But, Dad, it hurts me in a different place."

But all kidding aside, we are here tonight on serious business—the Lord's business. Jesus spent more time talking about stewardship of self and substance than about salvation. Salvation is not of lesser importance, but stewardship involves more than the salvation of souls—it involves the whole of Christian life.

This is why, without apology, I want to talk to you about stewardship. My text is found in Matthew 6:21: "For where your treasure is, there your heart will be also." It makes just as much sense when you turn it around: where your heart is, your treasure will be also.

—2—

Thanks, pastor, for your kind words of introduction. But, after all, you should say something nice about me. For I am here to talk to your church about giving more money.

A pastor once noticed that each Sunday someone would put an IOU in the collection plate. He figured this was simply a practical joke. But one Sunday there was an envelope containing enough bills to cover the previous IOUs. From then on the pastor watched the IOUs with great interest. They ranged all the way from five to twenty dollars—evidently based on what the giver thought the sermon was worth. But one Sunday the pastor received a slip of paper which read, "UO Me $5."

Seriously, however, stewardship involves more than

money. Money, yes! But stewardship encompasses all of life. I want to consider what Paul wrote about a collection to relieve the suffering believers in Jerusalem. Of the Macedonian Christians Paul said, ". . . they gave themselves first to the Lord and then to us in keeping with God's will" (2 Cor. 8:5).

—3—

Brother Chairman, while I realize that I cannot possibly live up to your glowing introduction, I will do my best. Your church will soon begin to collect pledges for next year's budget. If my remarks do not help you, I hope they will not hinder you in this effort.

Unfortunately, at such a gathering as this those who *need* to hear my words are not present. To invite them to a stewardship dinner is like sending a notice to rabbits to stay in their burrows the day you plan to go rabbit hunting.

Someone once said that there are three types of givers—the flint, the sponge, and the honeycomb. To get anything out of a flint you must hammer it. Even then you get mostly chips and sparks. To get water out of a sponge you must squeeze it. The harder you squeeze the more you get. But the honeycomb gets so full it overflows with sweetness. So I trust that the honeycombs will pass the word along to the flints and sponges.

You should look carefully to see which kind of giver you are. In Acts 20:35 Paul reminds the Ephesian elders, "[Remember] the words the Lord Jesus himself said: 'It is more blessed to give than to receive.' "

Let me introduce this text by borrowing some words from someone else.

God made the sun—it gives.
God made the moon—it gives.
God made the stars—they give.
God made the air—it gives.
God made the clouds—they give.
God made the earth—it gives.
God made the sea—it gives.
God made the trees—they give.
God made the flowers—they give.
God made the fowls—they give.
God made the beasts—they give.
God made the Plan—He gives.
God made man—he . . . ?

Each of us must answer this question for himself.

11

Responses to Convention Welcome

Religious Convention

My fellow laborers in Christ, it is my privilege and responsibility to respond on behalf of the _____ Convention/Conference/Synod to your superlative words of welcome.

Your city is well known as a gracious city. We have found this to be true. We are here because *you* wanted us—as demonstrated by your invitation. We are here because *we* want to be here—as evidenced by our acceptance of that invitation. When we leave we shall carry happy memories with us; and we will try to leave happy ones behind. Someone has said that hospitality should have no nature other than love. This may also be said of those who receive hospitality. So as guests and hosts we are bound together by the bonds of Christian love.

Needless to say, we live in a time which demands

the best that is in us—and that by the grace and power of God. Somewhere I read that "when the going gets tough the tough get going." Issues before us may be the occasion for differences of opinion, but they should be met in a spirit of unity. We shall debate without being adamant. We shall contend but not be contentious. We shall face crises with Christian courtesy. We shall decide issues without dividing fellowship. We shall so conduct ourselves that when we leave you will be glad that we came.

It is our prayer that our gathering here may be in the spirit of words written by Henry Wadsworth Longfellow:

> Where'er a noble deed is wrought,
> Where'er is spoken a noble thought,
>   Our hearts in glad surprise
>   To higher levels rise.

We need to follow the advice of the apostle Paul: ". . . whatever is true, whatever is noble, whatever is right, whatever is pure, whatever is lovely, whatever is admirable—if anything is excellent or praiseworthy—think about such things" (Phil. 4:8).

Political Convention

Mr. Chairman and my fellow delegates, it is an honor for me to speak on your behalf in response to the welcome of the Honorable _____, governor/mayor of the state/city of _____.

Mr. Governor/Mayor, let me express our appreciation for your gracious welcome. It is what we expected, for your state/city is well known for its warm

115

hospitality. In fact your welcome reminds me of a little verse by an unknown author:

Come in the evening, or come in the morning,
Come when you're looked for, or come without
warning;
Thousands of welcomes you'll find here before you.
And the oftener you come, the more we'll adore you.

We shall enjoy ourselves here. At the same time we are faced with some serious business—not that of our party alone but that of the entire nation/state. We will debate issues and make decisions. We will grapple with problems which concern the economic, political, and social well-being of our people. I do not need to stress the problems which beset our nation/state/world at this time. But we are confident that by facing these problems boldly and dealing with them realistically, we can at least move toward their solution. Thomas Carlyle reminds us that "in the huge mass of evil as it rolls and swells, there is ever some good working toward deliverance and triumphs."

In reciting the Pledge of Allegiance, we affirm "one nation, under God." We believe that as God has ordained the institution of government, in his providence he also guides history toward his intended goal. And he does so through men and women dedicated to doing his will. Reverend _____, who led our opening prayer, invoked the blessings of almighty God upon this convention. In that spirit I would like to read some words by F. J. Gilman:

God send us men whose aim will be
Not to defend some ancient creed,
But to live out the laws of Right
In every thought, and word and deed.

116

God send us men alert and quick
His lofty precepts to translate,
Until the laws of Christ become
The laws and habits of the State.
God send us men! God send us men!
Patient, courageous, strong and true;
With vision clear and mind equipped
His will to learn, His word to do.
God send us men with hearts ablaze,
All truth to love, all wrong to hate;
These are the patriots nations need,
These are the bulwarks of the State.

Convention of Attorneys

Mr. Chairman and my fellow delegates, on behalf of all of us I wish to express gratitude to the Honorable _____, president of the State Bar Association (or other appropriate title), for making us feel welcome and at home in this city.

We are dedicated to the cause of justice. The great Byzantine emperor Justinian I once said that "justice is the constant desire and effort to render to every man his due." The British statesman William E. Gladstone reminds us that "justice delayed is justice denied."

Justice is sometimes said to be blind: it does not grope and stumble through the world, but it is and/or should be applied without regard to party, kindred, or friendship. Our system of justice is based on law, not the whims of men.

Justice involves defense of the innocent as well as punishment of the guilty. But in both cases it must be exercised on the basis of truth. As Shakespeare writes:

> What stronger breastplate than a heart untainted!
> Thrice is he arm'd that hath his quarrel just,
> And he but naked, though locked up in steel,
> Whose conscience with injustice is corrupted.

It is our calling to sift truth from falsehood. We protect the rights of individuals and contribute to the successful operation of our government. It is to the furtherance and improvement of our profession that we are gathered here. May the God of all right bless us in our efforts.

Convention of Businessmen

Mr. President, may I speak briefly in response to the hearty welcome extended to us by Mayor _____ of this city? I trust that I may do so with sincerity. It is my hope that our coming here will benefit this city and contribute to the economic good of our nation.

The business community is constantly faced with new challenges and problems. How we react to them is the concern of every person attending this convention—and in that we are part of the international economic scene, this concern extends to every human being.

We must face our present challenges with optimistic realism. A fatal mistake of any contestant is to underestimate the strength of his opponent. However, it is equally fatal for him to approach the contest with

118

pessimism, defeatism, and the feeling that he cannot win.

We possess sufficient economic and intellectual power to solve the problems which face us. Someone has said that "the price of power is responsibility for the public good." So we should not approach this meeting selfishly, but altruistically.

Darwin P. Kingsley states it succinctly:

You have powers you never dreamed of. You can do things you never thought you could do. There are no limitations in what you can do except the limitations in your own mind as to what you cannot do. Don't think you cannot. Think you can.

Convention of Organized Labor

I am happy, Mr. Chairman, to speak for all of us in response to the fine welcome given to us by the Honorable Mr. _____, governor of the state of _____ (or another person and position).

We represent one of the greatest working forces in our nation. Someone has said, "The greatest asset of any nation is the spirit of its people, and the greatest danger that can menace any nation is the breakdown of that spirit—the will to win and the courage to work." In our organization we possess that spirit.

We have the will to win. A successful jockey, asked how he had won so many races, said that in the stretch he always whispered into his horse's ear,

> Roses are red, violets are blue,
> Horses that lose are made into glue.

In contrast, our will to win is due to more than the desire for self-preservation. We believe that when we succeed, the nation also succeeds. It is cooperative effort in every phase of industry which has made our nation great.

We also have the courage to work. The man who does only what is required of him is a slave; the truly free man is one who does more than what is required of him. He works for the joy of work and takes pride in what he produces. Someone once said that most footprints on the sands of time are made by work shoes, another that the clock-watcher will never become "the man of the hour."

Some people work with their brains, others with their hands. We work with both. We have not achieved our positions simply by learning the *tricks* of the trade, but by learning the trade itself. We are not satisfied with mediocrity. We are aware that if we do not find ways to improve our work, someone else will, and we will be the losers. No matter how excellent our skills may be, we know that there is no substitute for hard work.

Our organization has enabled us to pool our resources, to elevate ourselves from day laborers to a mighty force, and to make a great contribution to society. However, an organization is no more effective than the individuals of whom it is composed. Unless our demands for better working conditions and wages are backed up by better work, we are reduced to voices crying in the wilderness. Our power must not corrupt but construct, must not dominate but donate, must not simply wield a big stick but use better skills so that both labor and management will benefit.

In closing, let me remind you of a little prayer we were taught as children:

> Now I lay me down to sleep,
> I pray the Lord my soul to keep.
> If I should die before I wake,
> I pray the Lord my soul to take.

Someone has paraphrased this into a prayer for adults:

> Now I get me up to work,
> I pray the Lord I may not shirk.
> If I should die before tonight,
> I pray the Lord my work's all right.

Medical Convention

Mr. President and fellow physicians, I have been asked to respond to the warm welcome extended to us by our colleague, Dr. ＿＿＿＿＿＿, president of the local medical association.

We are all aware of the burden of responsibility we bear for the care of our patients. They place their confidence in us, and we must not betray that confidence. That is why we are here: to learn how we can serve our patients better.

Tremendous strides are being made by medical science; medical knowledge doubled five times during the first sixty years of this century. It now doubles every five years. However, this vast storehouse of new knowledge is of little or no use unless it is channeled through us to individual patients. Our profession faces many challenges, but none are more important than the learning of new skills and the sharpening of the ones we already possess. We have come here for this purpose. It is up to each of us to see that we have not come in vain.

News Convention

Mr. President, it is both an opportunity and responsibility to respond to the gracious welcome extended to us by Mr. _____, president of the local chamber of commerce. He reflects the warm spirit with which we have been greeted on every hand. We are happy to be here, and hope that our coming benefits your community.

An awesome power for good or evil is placed in the hands of the news media. Someone once noted that a drop of ink may make a million think. In this electronic age, to the drop of ink we must add the sound of the voice. We should never presume to think for people, yet we can guide their thinking in the right direction.

News reporting should deal with the facts, and leave interpretation to the editorial page. A noted Englishman, Sir Leslie Stephen, reminds us that "the only way in which one human can properly attempt to influence another is to encourage him to think for himself, instead of endeavoring to instill ready-made opinions into his head."

Freedom of the press is one of the most precious liberties granted to us by the Constitution. We must guard this freedom without abusing it. Four hundred years ago Martin Luther said, "We must throw the printer's inkpot at the devil." We must expose corruption and evil wherever they exist. However, our news reports should be more than cesspools of the sordid. They must also report the good things in life. Our audience needs to look beyond what is wrong to what is right in our nation.

As we deliberate upon matters pertaining to our field of endeavor, we need to preserve that delicate balance between responsibility and opportunity. Let us not shirk the one, let us seize the other.

General Convention

—1—

Mr. Mayor (or other appropriate title), we are grateful for your generous words of welcome. They reflect the spirit of all who have been responsible for the arrangements made for us.

Throughout your city, we keep seeing a little slogan: "Have a good day, and pass it on." It captures your optimism. However, while here, we hope to prove that we are not merely optimists but peptimists as well.

Somewhere I read the following:

> A pessimist says, "I don't think it can be done."
> An optimist says, "I'm sure there is a way."
> A peptimist says, "I just did it."

Someone else has written "The Pessimist's Creed."

> What's the use of sunshine? Only blinds your eyes.
> What's the use of knowledge? Only makes you wise.
> What's the use of smiling? Wrinkles up your face.
> What's the use of flowers? Clutter up the place.

What's the use of eating? Nothing—only taste.
What's the use of hustling? Haste is only waste.
What's the use of music? Just a lot of noise.
What's the use of loving? Only for the joys.
What's the use of singing? Only makes you glad.
What's the use of goodness when the whole world's
    bad?
What's the use of health? You might as well be sick.
What's the use of doing anything but kick?

In contrast, we hold an entirely different view of life. Ours is the attitude expressed in another slogan: "Cheer up! Today is the first day of the rest of your life!"

We are not unaware of the problems facing our generation, but see them as opportunities, as challenges. With all of us working together, we can solve these problems.

Speaking of the pessimist and optimist, I am reminded of a little poem about two frogs. I do not know who wrote it, but his message is both timely and timeless.

Two frogs fell into a deep cream bowl,
One was an optimistic soul,
But the other took the gloomy view,
"We shall drown," he cried without much ado!
So with a last despairing cry,
He flung up his legs and he said, "Good-by!"
Quoth the other frog with a merry grin,
"I can't get out, but I won't give in.
I'll just swim around till my strength is spent,
Then will I die the more content!"
Bravely he swam till it would seem,
His struggles began to churn the cream!

On the top of the butter at last he stopped,
And out of the bowl he gaily hopped!
What is the moral? 'Tis easily found:
If you can't hop out, keep swimming around!

Which "frog" are you?

—2—

Thank you for your wonderful words of welcome. Through them, you have set the tone for the entire convention.

I shall not speak of the agenda of business which is going to be followed. While that is important, there is another side to conventions—the delight in seeing old friends and the privilege of making new ones. So let us spend this time not on an onerous pilgrimage but on a delightful journey.

An anonymous poet tells us that

When life seems just a dreary grind,
  And things seem fated to annoy,
Say something nice to someone else
  And watch the world light up with joy.

Another writer says:

It takes so little to make us glad;
Just a cheering clasp of a friendly hand,
Just a word from one who can understand,
And we finish the task we long had planned,
And we lose the doubt and the fear we had—
So little it takes to make us glad.

To be sure, we all have our problems. We need to deal with them, not coddle them. This reminds me of the old man in a small Arkansas town who had many problems. One morning someone met him on the street and asked, "Uncle Billy, how are you this morning?" Uncle Billy replied, "Well, first of all, tell me if you have time to listen."

If you have problems and you need to talk about them, some of us will have time to listen. However, if they can wait, there is a far better way to spend your leisure time during this convention, expressed by an anonymous writer:

> Build yourself a strong box,
>   Fashion each part with care;
> Fit it with hasp and padlock,
>   Put all your troubles there.
> Hide therein all your failures,
>   And each bitter cup you quaff,
> Lock all your heartaches within it,
>   Then—sit on the lid and laugh!
>
> Tell no one of its contents.
>   Never its secret share;
> Drop in your cares and worries,
>   Keep them forever there,
> Hide them from sight so completely,
>   The world will never dream half.
> Fasten the top down securely,
>   Then—sit on the lid and laugh!

12

Responses to Introductions

Minister as Civic Club Speaker

Thank you, Mr. Chairman, for your generous words of introduction, and for the privilege of being your speaker today. It is good to be with friends and comrades-in-arms in building a better city.

None of us is as good as he can and ought to be. However, I hope we *can* say, "I am better today than I was yesterday, but not as good as I expect to be tomorrow." Coué claimed that "every day in every way I am getting better and better." However, we must add "by the grace of God." Actually, we are all *being* and *becoming:* what we are tomorrow, we are becoming today.

You invite speakers to your club because you feel that they have something to say to you. As a pastor, I am qualified to speak about religion and morals. So I will center my message—call it a sermon, if you like—on that area.

127

Former President James A. Garfield once said, "I mean to make myself a man, and if I succeed in that, I shall succeed in everything." With this thought in mind, and against the background of *being* and *becoming*, I want to reflect on Paul's words in Philippians 3:13: "[This] one thing I do."

Minister as Chamber of Commerce Speaker

Mr. Chairman, I appreciate your gracious words of welcome. I should be thanking *you* for this privilege. For where else in this city could I find an audience like this? You are the dynamic force that makes our city move. In the past, men like you have carved out great cities from small villages. Now you are proving to be their worthy successors as you build for a greater tomorrow.

Like so many other large cities, ours is involved in urban renewal. Millions of dollars are being invested to change ghetto neighborhoods into a thriving economic community.

As a pastor, I see this as a parable of life. You are renewing the heart of the city because you realize that this is necessary for the well-being of the rest of the community's body. This requires many dedicated people.

In one of G. K. Chesterton's poems, he describes a crew of men wrecking an old building. Chesterton asks the foreman if these men could *build* a building. The foreman says no, adding that common labor is able to wreck in a couple of days what builders have taken years to do. Then the poem continues:

I asked myself, as I went my way,
"Which of these roles have I tried today?
Am I a builder who works with care,
Measuring life by the rule and square,
Shaping my deeds by a well made plan,
Patiently doing the best I can?
Or am I a wrecker who walks the town,
Content with the labor of tearing down?"

You are rebuilding the heart of the city, but what about the city's heart? In a far deeper sense a city's spiritual state contributes more to its rise or ruin than anything else. No city is greater than the character of its people.

Why build these cities glorious
If man unbuilded goes?
In vain we build the world, unless
The builder also grows.

—*Anonymous*

King Solomon was a great builder, but in Psalm 127:1 he acknowledges, "Unless the LORD builds the house, its builders labor in vain. Unless the LORD watches over the city, the watchmen stand guard in vain."

Speaker at a Boys' Club Banquet

Mr. Chairman, I appreciate your kind words of introduction. It is good to be in a group so full of possibilities. Men are what they are, but a boy is what he may become; the word *impossible* is not in his vocabulary.

A teacher took her grade-school class on a tour of

the White House. The next day she asked the children to write about their impressions of the tour. One boy wrote, "I was glad to have the opportunity to visit my future home." We may laugh at what he wrote, but he may have been telling the truth. For there is no limit to the possibilities of what a boy may become.

A university president had the habit of tipping his hat to every boy he met. When asked why, he replied, "I never know when I am speaking to a future president of the United States."

Somewhere in this great land of ours are boys who will someday be our presidents. Even if you are not a future president, you are a future *something.* You may be a future businessman, doctor, lawyer, preacher, farmer, scientist, athlete, or musician. You must decide *now* to be the best you can be, and you must start today, not tomorrow. Abraham Lincoln went from a log cabin to the White House. Listen to what *he* said: "I will study and get ready and the opportunity will come."

Boys grow into men. What kind of a man will *you* be? I am not a preacher, but I want to talk to you for a few minutes about a twelve-year-old boy who became the greatest man who ever lived. Can you tell me who he was? Well, let me tell you. "And Jesus grew in wisdom and stature, and in favor with God and men" (Luke 2:52).

Speaker at a Girls' Club Banquet

Thank you for your kind words of introduction. I do not intend to make a speech; I want to have a heart-to-heart talk with you, for I am a girl like you. I am older than you in years, but at heart I am still a girl. The fact that I have lived a little longer than you have may help me to say some things that will be helpful to you as you grow up. I am going to do so by telling you a true story.

Many years ago a baby girl became very sick. She eventually recovered. In fact, she looked like any other baby girl, but she was not. Her illness had left her deaf, dumb, and blind: she could not hear, she could not speak, she could not see.

Her family found a woman to look after her, to be her companion and teacher. No one had been able to communicate with her. However, her teacher discovered a way of talking to her by tapping in the girl's hand. One of the first things the teacher told her about was God. The girl told her teacher-companion, "I always knew about him; I just did not know his name."

This method of communication was eventually used with other handicapped people. In spite of her problems, this girl became a blessing to others. She eventually became a writer, and with her teacher's help, she lectured.

Oh, I almost forgot to tell you her name! She was Helen Keller. The world is a richer place because she lived. I think a few quotations from her will show you what I mean.

She had every reason to doubt, but listen to what she says about *faith*.

Dark as my path may seem to others, I carry a magic light in my heart. Faith, the spiritual strong searchlight illumines the way, and although sinister doubts lurk in the shadow, I walk unafraid toward the Enchanted Wood where the foliage is always green, where joy abides, where nightingales nest and sing, and where life and death are one in the presence of the Lord.

She could have been a pessimist, but listen to how *optimistic* she was:

Keep your face to the sunshine and you cannot see the shadows.

Helen Keller knew *sorrow*, but she rose above it to comfort others.

This world is so full of care and sorrow that it is a gracious debt we owe to one another to discover the bright crystals of delight hidden in somber circumstances and irksome tasks.

If Helen Keller could overcome her handicaps and become such a blessing to the world, surely with our many abilities we can do no less.

Church Business Administrator

Brother Moderator, at the request of the program committee of our association/conference/synod, I am here to speak about my work as a church business administrator. Of course, my responsibility is to look after the business affairs of the church according to the policies set by the congregation and implemented by various church committees. Today, however, I shall focus on stewardship.

Some figures taken from the *Southern Baptist Handbook* indicate that the practice of stewardship is a lost art. The average American spends only five cents a day for religious and welfare causes. In contrast, he spends nine cents for tobacco, fifteen cents for alcoholic beverages, twenty-two cents for recreation, fifty-eight cents for transportation (including foreign travel), fifty-nine cents for taxes, one dollar and twelve cents for food, and two dollars and thirty cents for other household expenses (rent, clothing, savings, medical, miscellaneous).

However, there is another type of stewardship which is often overlooked—the stewardship of administering tithes and donations. Churches should be careful to see that people's gifts are used for the purposes for which they are given, and that the church remains solvent. My duty, under the direction of the finance committee, lies here more than in any other area.

While I am not a preacher, it is fitting at this point for me to point out biblical guidelines for the sound management of funds given for the Lord's work. Paul was taking an offering in the churches of Galatia, Macedonia, and Greece to send to suffering Christians in Palestine. After spelling out how the money was to be received, he writes the following to the church in Corinth: "Then, when I arrive, I will give letters of introduction to the men you approve and send them with your gift to Jerusalem. If it seems advisable for me to go also, they will accompany me" (1 Cor. 16:3–4).